T0316517

Cambridge Elements ≡

Elements in Applied Social Psychology
edited by
Susan Clayton
College of Wooster, Ohio

IDENTITY DEVELOPMENT DURING STEM INTEGRATION FOR UNDERREPRESENTED MINORITY STUDENTS

Sophie L. Kuchynka
Rutgers University, Newark, New Jersey
Alexander E. Gates
Rutgers University, Newark, New Jersey
Luis M. Rivera
Rutgers University, Newark, New Jersey

CAMBRIDGE
UNIVERSITY PRESS

CAMBRIDGE
UNIVERSITY PRESS

University Printing House, Cambridge CB2 8BS, United Kingdom

One Liberty Plaza, 20th Floor, New York, NY 10006, USA

477 Williamstown Road, Port Melbourne, VIC 3207, Australia

314–321, 3rd Floor, Plot 3, Splendor Forum, Jasola District Centre,
New Delhi – 110025, India

79 Anson Road, #06–04/06, Singapore 079906

Cambridge University Press is part of the University of Cambridge.

It furthers the University's mission by disseminating knowledge in the pursuit of education, learning, and research at the highest international levels of excellence.

www.cambridge.org
Information on this title: www.cambridge.org/9781108794787
DOI: 10.1017/9781108882071

First published 2020

A catalogue record for this publication is available from the British Library.

ISBN 978-1-108-79478-7 Paperback
ISSN 2631-777X (online)
ISSN 2631–7761 (print)

Cambridge University Press has no responsibility for the persistence or accuracy of URLs for external or third-party internet websites referred to in this publication and does not guarantee that any content on such websites is, or will remain, accurate or appropriate.

Identity Development during STEM Integration for Underrepresented Minority Students

Elements in Applied Social Psychology

DOI: 10.1017/9781108882071
First published online: October 2020

Sophie L. Kuchynka
Rutgers University, Newark, New Jersey

Alexander E. Gates
Rutgers University, Newark, New Jersey

Luis M. Rivera
Rutgers University, Newark, New Jersey

Authors for correspondence: Sophie L. Kuchynka, sk2224@psychology.rutgers.edu, Luis M. Rivera, Luis@psychology.rutgers.edu

Abstract: Over the past three decades, research efforts and interventions have been implemented across the United States to increase the persistent underrepresentation of minority (URM) students in science, technology, engineering, and math (STEM). This Element systematically compares STEM interventions that offer resources and opportunities related to mentorship, research, and more. We organize the findings of this literature into a multiphase framework of STEM integration and identity development. We propose four distinct phases of STEM integration: Phase 1: High School; Phase 2: Pre-College Summer; Phase 3: College First Year; and Phase 4: College Second Year through Graduation. We combine tenets of theories about social identity, stereotypes and bias, and the five-factor operationalization of identity formation to describe each phase of STEM integration. Findings indicate the importance of exploration through exposure to STEM material, mentorship, and diverse STEM communities. We generalize lessons from STEM interventions to URM students across institutions.

Keywords: STEM Pathways, STEM leaky pipeline, STEM interventions, STEM Belonging, Mentorship

ISBNs: 9781108794787 (PB), 9781108882071 (OC)
ISSNs: 2631-777X (online), ISSN 2631–7761 (print)

Contents

1 Introduction

The United States faces a pressing need to fill nearly one million new science, technology, engineering, and math (STEM) jobs over the next decade (Fayer, Lacey, & Watson, 2017). Not only will STEM jobs remain underfilled at current STEM graduation rates, but these rates are also disproportionately lower among Black, Latinx, and Native American students when compared with White and Asian students (Fayer et al., 2017; National Science Foundation, 2019). Adults from underrepresented minority (URM) groups account for 35 percent of the United States population, but they only earn 24 percent of STEM bachelor's degrees, 23 percent of STEM master's degrees, and 15 percent of STEM doctoral degrees (National Science Foundation, 2019). Moreover, URM students are more likely than non-URM students to exit STEM majors (Graham, Frederick, Byars-Winston, Hunter, & Handelsman, 2013; Griffith, 2010); when do they earn STEM degrees, URM students are less likely than non-URM students to go to graduate school (Allen-Ramdial & Campbell, 2014). Altogether, the data suggest that the United States is losing qualified and talented URM individuals, thus maintaining a mostly homogenous STEM workforce.

When URM students choose STEM pathways, multiple societal benefits follow. First, increasing STEM graduation rates among URM groups can ameliorate economic ramifications of the labor shortages in STEM (National Science Board, 2015). Second, it helps the United States remain a global leader and competitor in STEM innovation (Griffith, 2010; Hulton, 2019; National Academies of Science, 2007; National Science Board, 2015). Third, increasing diversity in STEM fields improves scientific innovation and business performance through the diversity of perspectives (Lee & Buxton, 2010; Richard, 2000). For example, ethnic-racial diversity in teams improves collective strategizing leading to institutional competitive advantages (Richard, 2000). Finally, opportunity, access, and participation in high-status STEM fields (e.g., engineering, academia) are fundamental to increasing ethnic-racial equity (Lacy, 2015). These four benefits coalesce to address and improve social and economic justice in the United States.

The trend of increased URM attrition in STEM degrees and careers is known metaphorically as the *STEM leaky pipeline*, which generally refers to how URMs and women, when compared with non-URMs and men, respectively, are "leaked" at each juncture of STEM educational and career trajectories (Berryman, 1983). However, researchers and practitioners have recently recommended replacing the metaphor with *STEM pathways* to emphasize the importance of being intentional when providing high-quality education and training opportunities to URMs (National Science Board, 2015). Consistent with this shift, research is focusing less on person-based deficits – understanding why URM students as individuals are not pursuing advanced STEM degrees – and more on the role of structural and contextual factors that ensure access to quality STEM education, research, and mentorship opportunities that promote the pursuit of a successful STEM career (National Science Board, 2015).

The lack of URMs in STEM fields is rooted in historic systems of stratification, namely institutional discrimination, negative cultural stereotypes, less access to opportunities, and lack of encouragement to pursue STEM (Braddock & McPartland, 1987; Oakes, 1990). Researchers continue to seek the best structural strategies to increase access to high-quality STEM education and training among URMs (National Science Board, 2015; National Science Foundation, 2005). Accordingly, wide-ranging intervention efforts have been introduced and tested over the past three decades (National Academies of Science, 2007; National Science Foundation, 2005). Although many STEM interventions aim to increase STEM participation among all college students, a subset is tailored to increase URM student recruitment and retention. Despite intervention efforts to get URM students on STEM pathways, minimal gains, at best, have been achieved (National Science Foundation, 2019).

For URM students, STEM disciplines pose unique obstacles. White and Asian (non-URM) students and faculty members are overrepresented in STEM fields (National Science Foundation, 2019; Rendón, Garcia, & Person, 2004). Relatedly, and probably consequently, URM students in STEM frequently report feelings of isolation (Grossman & Porsche, 2014; Malone & Barbino, 2009; Seymour & Hewitt, 1997), lack of effective mentorship (Pfund, Byars-Winston, Branchaw, Hurtado, & Eagan, 2016), and subtle (Brown et al., 2016) and overt (Rankin & Reason, 2005; Swim, Hyers, Cohen, Fitzgerald, & Bylsma, 2003) experiences of bias. Indeed, URM students often associate the STEM campus climate with negative ethnic-racial experiences (Hurtado & Carter, 1997; Johnson, 2012; Strayhorn, 2015).

Equally important, STEM disciplines pose additional challenges that coexist with ethnicity and race, namely, that URM students tend to be first-generation college students and come from low-socioeconomic families (Allen-Ramdial & Campbell, 2014; Choy, 2001; McCarron & Inkelas, 2006). First-generation college students often experience weaker integration into college environments and are retained at lower rates due in part to the lack of social capital transmitted by their families (Atherton, 2014). Parents of first-generation college students did not attend college, so they are unable to communicate higher education norms, expectations, and experiences to their children. As it relates to socioeconomic factors, URM students are more likely to come from high schools that are underfunded and lack resources (The Commonwealth Institute, 2016). High schools that predominately serve URM students are less likely to offer advanced STEM courses, have proper research equipment and updated textbooks, and have an adequate student-teacher ratio (The Commonwealth Institute, 2016). Experiencing one or a combination of these obstacles and challenges undermines a sense of belonging in STEM, STEM identity, and integration into STEM, which are all theorized to influence STEM persistence and success (Chang et al., 2014; Wang, 2013).

2 About This Element

This Element evaluates STEM interventions that sought to increase STEM recruitment, retention, and persistence among URM students in high schools and colleges across the United States. We focus on the United States because it has an increasingly diverse culture with an unparalleled history of intergroup dynamics that persist today, and the country's ethnic-racial marginalized groups underrepresented in STEM face a unique set of structural barriers and challenges rooted in historic and systemic racism. Also, the United States predicted a "STEM crisis" (National Science Foundation, 2005) that resulted in significant public and private funding of STEM interventions nationally over the past two decades. This provides a unique opportunity to systematically evaluate URM experiences in STEM interventions across the United States.

This Element evaluates STEM interventions that provide insight into the relation between structural and contextual factors and psychological processes – specifically, opportunities for wide-ranging STEM exposure, participation in STEM communities, and mentorship relationships and their relation to STEM identity development and integration. There is variability in the theoretical frameworks that researchers apply to their STEM interventions, if they apply any theory at all. We evaluate STEM identity development among URMs through the perspectives of social psychology theories, namely, social identity theory (Tajfel, 1981; Tajfel & Turner, 1979, 1986; Turner & Reynolds, 2011) and the stereotype inoculation model (Dasgupta, 2011). Also, we draw from Erickson's theory of identity development (Erikson, 1968) and its extension, the five-dimension model of identity formation (Luyckx et al., 2006, 2008) to classify and explain the STEM integration process.

3 STEM Identity Development and Integration

STEM identity is the social cognitive association between the self and (a) STEM disciplines (Dennehy & Dasgupta, 2017; Kuchynka, Reifsteck, Gates, & Rivera, 2020) and (b) the groups of individuals in STEM disciplines (e.g., advanced students, academics, industry professionals; McDonald, Zeigler-Hill, Vrabel, & Escobar, 2019; Starr, 2018). STEM identity is further moderated by how central and important group membership in STEM is to one's self-concept (e.g., "being a STEM student is an important part of my self-image"; Ramsey, Betz, & Sekaquaptewa, 2013) and by how typical one appraises oneself as a group member (e.g., "I feel like I'm just like people who are good at STEM"; McDonald et al., 2019; Starr, 2018). We focus on STEM identity because it is a consistent social cognitive predictor of STEM performance outcomes (Chen et al., 2020; Hernandez, Schultz, Estrada, Woodcock, & Chance, 2013). Among URM students, strong STEM identities are related to higher STEM grades, higher retention and graduation rates, and greater persistence in and commitment to STEM even after college graduation (Chemers et al., 2011; Estrada et al., 2018; Estrada, Woodcock, Hernandez, & Schultz, 2011). Given these achievements, developing and maintaining a strong STEM identity are especially important in URM students because they encounter unique obstacles in STEM settings (Brown et al., 2016; Rankin & Reason, 2005; Strayhorn, 2015; Swim et al., 2003). URM students often report negative ethnic-racial experiences in STEM because of cultural stereotypes (Chang et al., 2011; Grossman & Porche, 2014), which can lead to dis-identification to protect their self-image (Major et al. 1998), and to high rates of STEM attrition (Beasley & Fischer, 2012).

Connected to STEM identity development is STEM integration. Academic integration is broadly conceptualized as the degree to which a student participates in university culture inside and outside the classroom (Davidson & Wilson, 2013; Tinto, 1975, 1987, 1988). We refer to STEM integration as the formal academic and the informal social behavioral participation in STEM. Formal academic aspects include, but are not limited to, taking STEM classes, joining research labs, attending conferences, delivering presentations, and mentorship. The informal social aspects include, but are not limited to, extracurricular activities, study groups, and casual interactions with peers and faculty. Weaker integration in STEM results in higher STEM exit rates among URM students compared with non-URM students (Estrada et al., 2011), but this inequality can be reduced with greater STEM integration (Mahoney & Cairns, 1997). STEM identities and STEM integration develop simultaneously and are synergistic, which is consistent with the fundamental social psychological hypothesis that cognitions influence behaviors, but behaviors influence cognitions (for a review, see Fazio & Zanna, 1981). Therefore, a feedback loop exists between STEM identity and integration, each exerting mutually reinforcing effects.

3.1 Social Identity Theory

Social psychological theories on social group membership provide a lens through which to understand STEM identity development. The social self consists of multiple identities that include social (race/ethnicity, gender), professional (career), and intimate (family, friends) categories (Brewer, 1991). STEM identity represents a distinct, professional group membership developed through cognitively associating the self with STEM group members and STEM disciplines (Dennehy & Dasgupta, 2017; McDonald et al., 2019). When professional identities become central to the self, they function as a source of motivation to achieve long-term goals and aid in short-term persistence, particularly in challenging domains (Eccles, 2009). Students who hold STEM central to their self-concept subsequently reap the functional benefits of professional group identification.

Social identity theory suggests that the self-concept consists of one's personal identity and one's social identity (Tajfel, 1978, 1981; Tajfel & Turner, 1979, 1986). Personal identity is the individual self, defined by important and distinct individual attributes. By comparison, social identity is the collective self, defined by group memberships and important and distinct group attributes. Depending on the situation, individuals will self-categorize with either their social or their personal identity (Turner et al., 1987). Social (group) identities are often activated in situations that require an individual to interact with ingroup versus outgroup members (Tajfel, 1982; Tajfel & Turner, 1979).

Because individuals develop a positive emotional attachment to their social groups (Tajfel, 1979; Turner, Reynolds, Haslam, & Veenstra, 2006), social identities can be a source of belonging and value (Swann & Bosson, 2010). Individuals need to feel socially connected to and have positive emotions toward a group to incorporate group membership into their self-concept. These social identity components are constructed through interactions with group members who exhibit the cognitive elements of identity (e.g., ingroup stereotypes) through group-based consensus (Postmes, Baray, Haslam, Morton, & Swaab, 2006). Individual group members need to perceive the commonalities among the collective perspectives of the ingroup rooted in a shared social reality (Ashforth & Mael, 1989). Further, group leaders exert an especially strong influence through their individual actions; their verbal and nonverbal communications with ingroup members continuously inform the content of social identity (Hogg & Reid, 2006).

Social identity researchers further distinguish between identity centrality and identity typicality (Leach et al., 2008; Wilson, & Leaper, 2016). Identity centrality is how important and valued a group membership is to one's self-concept (Tajfel

& Turner, 1986). Identity typicality is the perception of oneself as a prototypical group member (Leach et al., 2008; Wilson & Leaper, 2016) and highlights the need to feel recognized and accepted as a member of a social group (Kim, Sinatra, & Seyranian, 2018). Both identity centrality and identity typicality are important to a sense of belonging to, and feeling accepted by, a group and its community (Ashforth & Mael, 1989; Carlone & Johnson, 2007; Kim, Sinatra, & Seyranian, 2018; Postmes et al., 2006).

As applied to STEM identity development, social identity theory implies that incoming students need to first learn the content – beliefs, norms, roles, stereotypes – of the STEM group and disciplines and then associate these components with their self-concept (Herrera, Hurtado, Garcia, & Gasiewski, 2012). During this process, students also need to form a sense of belonging to a STEM community – to feel connected to and accepted by other STEM group members (Carlone & Johnson, 2007; Kim, Sinatra, & Seyranian, 2018; Lewis, 2003). Indeed, perceptions of group support predict identification with academic domains over time (Bizumic, Reynolds, & Meyers, 2012), feeling accepted by a STEM community facilitates academic and social adjustment (Ostrove & Long, 2007), and being recognized as a scientist by fellow scientists is particularly important for URM women (Carlone & Johnson, 2007). Because of the importance of acceptance and recognition, STEM identity researchers interested in URM group members highlight identity typicality because it is challenged by cultural stereotypes that portray non-URM groups of people as more "fit" for STEM (Starr, 2018). Taken together, these findings highlight the need for a welcoming STEM community to facilitate STEM identity development among new URM students.

Social identity development also involves intergroup comparisons (Oakes, Haslam, & Turner, 1994). Individuals often compare the behaviors, interests, and values of the ingroup with those of outgroups and conclude that their own behaviors, interests, and values align more closely with the ingroup. Intergroup comparisons result in ingroup favoritism. Though ingroup favoritism often has negative consequences in the contexts of prejudice and discrimination (Brewer, 1999; Crocker & Schwartz, 1985), it may benefit URM students' identification with STEM. As students integrate into STEM, they may develop stronger preferences toward their majors and ingroup members, compared with alternative majors and outgroup members, respectively. Ingroup favoritism may work in tandem with STEM identity development to solidify students' status as STEM group members. To illustrate, individuals in general exhibit a stronger implicit association between STEM and men relative to women, but female STEM group members actually demonstrate a stronger implicit association between STEM and women relative to men (Farrell & McHugh, 2017, 2020), suggesting that ingroup favoritism can develop even among marginalized and underrepresented groups in STEM.

Notably, forming a STEM identity need not come at the expense of other central social identities such as ethnic-racial identities. In fact, maintaining multiple group memberships and identities benefits the process of transitioning to a new social identity, because they provide psychological resources to cope with stressful life changes (Iyer, Jetten, Tsivrikos, Postmes, & Haslam, 2009). However, as noted earlier, STEM identity development presents obstacles for URMs who face pervasive cultural stereotypes that portray their ethnic-racial (and gender for women) identity as incompatible with STEM (Eaton, Saunders, Jacobson, & West, 2020; Starr, 2018). Being in an environment where one's social group is stereotyped can lead URMs to diminish the importance of an identity or push them to find alternative environments that are more inclusive (Deaux, 1994). In STEM, URMs may either disregard their ethnic-racial identity to "fit in" or leave STEM to find other more accepting domains. However, we posit in this Element that URM STEM students do not need to relinquish their ethnic-racial identity to succeed or belong in STEM. Academic and professional settings that are inclusive and diverse expand the STEM prototype and facilitate STEM identity development in URM students without diminishing the centrality of their ethnic-racial identity.

STEM stereotypes also exacerbate belonging uncertainty, the concern about one's social acceptance (Walton & Cohen, 2007). Because URMs are more likely to experience a lack of fit in STEM, any perceived threat to belonging results in a variety of negative downstream consequences including reduced motivation (Walton & Cohen, 2007). Coping with perceived threats to social belonging among URM students in STEM promotes higher academic achievement and well-being (Walton & Cohen, 2011). However, fear of confirming negative STEM stereotypes often leads URMs to underperform (Steele, 1997). These stereotype threat experiences lead to domain dis-identification over time (Woodcock et al., 2012). Therefore, identity belongingness concerns are important to understanding URM student experiences in STEM environments.

3.2 Stereotype Inoculation Model

To combat STEM stereotypes, the stereotype inoculation model proposes that in-group peers and mentors serve as a "social vaccine" and function to increase social belonging (Dasgupta, 2011; Stout et al., 2011). URM students may feel like imposters in STEM due to their historic and continued underrepresentation, leading to divergence between their self-concept and STEM. URM students may doubt their ability and performance because of subtle and sometimes overt cues that they do not fit with the prototypic representation of a STEM group member. URM students inoculate themselves against these barriers by forming relationships with other URM STEM group members. Observing nonprototypical or exemplar ingroup members can enable students to imagine their future self achieving specific goals (Markus & Nurius, 1986; Morgenroth, Ryan, & Peters, 2015). URM STEM exemplars diverge from the STEM prototype and demonstrate that someone from a similar background can achieve success in STEM. Peers and mentors are two primary types of STEM group members who serve as STEM exemplars.

3.2.1 Peers

Since social identities develop from incorporating the prototypic representations of the ingroup into the self-concept (Turner et al., 1994), it is important for URM students to be surrounded by URM STEM peers (Dasgupta, 2011). URM peers inoculate one another against the harms of STEM stereotypes. However, the salience of the numeric underrepresentation of URM groups often results in URM students feeling out of place and overly visible (Bodenhausen, 2010). Frequent exposure to diverse peers in STEM contexts alters the STEM prototype of White and Asian men by making URM STEM group members chronically salient. Thus, immersion into a diverse STEM community of peers facilitates the perception of overlap between the self and other STEM ingroup members (Dasgupta, 2011; Dasgupta & Stout, 2014).

3.2.2 Mentors

Similar to peers, mentors promote positive psychological and professional outcomes (Allen, Eby, & Lentz, 2006). According to mentoring theories, mentor-mentee relationship quality refers to the affective relationship components respect, trust, and connectedness that subsequently facilitate mentees' professional identification and competence (Kram, 1985; Ragins, 2012). Effective mentors in STEM provide professional support (e.g., academic goal support) and psychosocial support (e.g., trust and emotional support; National Academies of Sciences, Engineering, and Medicine, 2019), and they role model ingroup values, goals, and behaviors, inspiring mentees to follow suit (Morgenroth, Ryan, & Peters, 2015).

Mentors in STEM can be upper-level undergraduate students, graduate students, faculty members, or industry professionals. Mentors provide access to STEM-related opportunities and improve STEM outcomes such as grade performance among mentees (Haeger & Fresquez, 2016). Unsurprisingly, lack of or low-quality mentorship is consistently identified as a main contributor to URM STEM attrition (Beasley & Fischer, 2012; Maton, Hrabowski, & Ozdemir, 2007). Some evidence even suggests that quality, not quantity, of interactions with faculty mentors predicts success (e.g., Foertsch, Alexander, & Penberthy, 2000). Therefore, mentors who wish to build a strong relationship need to pay close attention to the mentees' psychological and social needs. Ultimately, positive mentor experiences predict URM integration into STEM (Anderson & Kim, 2006; Byars-Winston et al., 2015; Estrada et al., 2018; Lisberg & Woods, 2018).

The type of mentorship that promotes the strongest STEM identity and academic persistence is still under investigation. However, a new conceptualization of mentoring coined "near-peer" mentoring emphasizes the importance of providing mentees with a mentor who is slightly more advanced in their educational or career trajectory (Malik, 2014; Tenenbaum et al., 2014; Trujillo et al., 2015; Wilson & Grigorian, 2019). The "nearness" in educational and maturity levels is theorized to have a number of benefits for the mentee such as developing STEM-based skills (Quitadamo, Brahler, & Crouch, 2009), promoting STEM interest (Wilson & Grigorian, 2019), and even increasing STEM retention (Watkins & Mazur, 2013). Near-peer mentors also reap benefits including stronger self-efficacy and science identity (Trujillo et al., 2015). Near-peer mentoring may be particularly important for URM students because, as described earlier, they lack ingroup exemplars in STEM and there are not enough URM faculty to mentor URM students (Rendón, Garcia, & Person, 2004). Also, near-peer mentors promote social belonging (Trujillo et al., 2015), a concern among marginalized groups in STEM (Walton & Cohen, 2007, 2011).

3.3 Developmental Processes Underlying Identity

While social identity theory explains the cognitive, affective, and behavioral processes related to group membership, Erikson's (1968) theory on identity formation focuses on the developmental process of identity at different phases of exploration and commitment. According to Erikson, identity formation reflects a continuous process throughout adolescence and young adulthood in which an individual weighs alternative social information to examine which identities match their interests and goals. Even after an individual makes a commitment to a future goal, they will continue the process of evaluating alternatives to strengthen their corresponding identity. Erikson (1963) emphasized identity versus role confusion (i.e., uncertainty about one's place in society) that arises during late adolescence, marking the onset of exploring what roles adolescents will occupy as adults.

Building on Erikson's theory on identity formation, Luyckx and colleagues (2006, 2008) operationalized five dimensions of identity development. The first two dimensions reflect two types of exploration: breadth and depth. Exploration in breadth focuses on the preliminary gathering of information to weigh potential alternatives to begin making commitments. Exploration in depth pertains to gathering additional information; communicating with ingroup members about the content of the identity; and evaluating whether their existing commitments are compatible with their personal values, interests, and goals. The third dimension is commitment making, which refers to making specific choices, and the fourth is identification with commitment, which reflects the degree of identification with those choices. Once people achieve identification with commitment, they experience a host of positive outcomes including superior decision-making abilities and higher levels of well-being (Kunnen et al., 2008; Schwartz, 2001). Finally, the fifth dimension is ruminative exploration, which is characterized by indecisiveness and hesitation. Ruminative exploration is distinct from the other dimensions in that it involves maladaptive tendencies associated with higher depressive symptoms stemming from feeling confused and overwhelmed from perceiving limitless career options (Luyckx et al., 2008).

3.4 Summary

Based on the theories reviewed here, we posit that stronger and more stable STEM identities among URM students will result from experiencing three components during STEM integration. First, students should be immersed in a diverse STEM community of peers. Second, students should receive diverse, high-quality mentorship from multiple sources. Both a community of peers and high-quality mentorship operate throughout STEM integration to combat cultural stereotypes and change STEM prototypes. Finally, students should have the opportunity to thoroughly explore varied potential alternatives and commitments. Exploration should occur early and include varied exposure to STEM to begin the iterative cycles of evaluating multiple alternatives that then narrow in scope with each integration phase. Overall, placing URM students in academic contexts that include these components should support the development of a strong and stable STEM identity, including identity typicality and centrality. The interventions presented in this Element provide evidence for these components and their interrelations, which are displayed in Figure 1.

4 Four Phases of URM Students' Identity and Integration

Drawing from the above review, we propose that STEM identity development is a process that unfolds across distinct phases of exploration and commitment

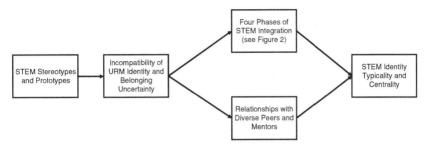

Figure 1 Pathways among identity compatibility, typicality, and centrality, mediated by STEM integration and diverse peers and mentorship for URM students.

making that occur throughout integration into STEM. As displayed in Figure 2, we classify four phases that emphasize varying degrees of exploration and commitment making. Phase 1: *High School* largely consists of initial exploration in breadth, whereas Phase 2: *Pre-College Summer* focuses on continued exploration in breadth, initial commitment making, and initial exploration in depth. Phase 3: *College First Year* emphasizes continued exploration in depth and continued commitment making. Finally, Phase 4: *College Second Year through Graduation* focuses on preventing ruminative exploration through promoting adaptive exploration tendencies. These tendencies are actualized via final exploration in depth and final commitment making. Ultimately, *full integration* is achieved. The four phases are dynamic and synergistic, and they influence URM students' STEM identity.

4.1 STEM Interventions Inclusion Criteria

We identify and review URM STEM interventions and organize them into the four phases outlined in Figure 2. STEM interventions administer a wide variety of measures, but, consistent with our previous review, we include those that assess at least one of the following social psychological variables: STEM identity, self-efficacy, STEM interest, sense of belonging, and STEM intentions. We define each variable as follows:

- *STEM identity*, as discussed earlier, includes the cognitive associations between the self and STEM disciplines and group members; these associations are further moderated by identity centrality and typicality. STEM identity is our main social psychological construct because it represents a primary predictor of URM STEM performance and persistence.
- *Self-efficacy* is the degree to which an individual believes they have the ability and talent to accomplish certain tasks (Bandura, 1986). Self-efficacy is an

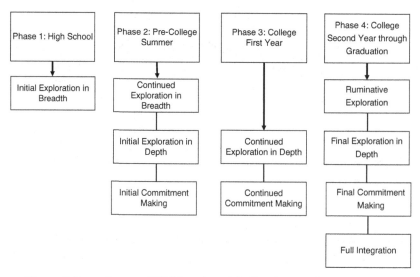

Figure 2 Four phases of URM students' STEM integration and identity.

important predictor of academic retention (Raelin et al., 2015), STEM persistence among URM and non-URM students (Lent et al., 2016), and STEM goals among URM students (Byars-Winston, Estrada, Howard, Davis, & Zalapa, 2010).

- *STEM interest* is the desire to engage with domain-specific material and the affective states of attitudes, liking, and attraction associated with engagement (Hidi & Renninger, 2006; Renninger, 2009; Valsiner, 1992). STEM interest is related to STEM persistence among URM and non-URM students (Lent et al., 2016).
- *Sense of belonging* represents the degree to which individuals feel socially connected, which is central to motivation (Baumeister & Leary, 1995). Applied to an academic context, sense of belonging is defined as feeling accepted, valued, and supported by the STEM community and its members (e.g., peers, faculty members; Strayhorn, 2018). Sense of belonging predicts STEM identity (Kuchynka, Findley-Van Nostrand, & Pollenz, 2019), academic performance (Chen et al., 2020; Freeman, Anderman, & Jensen, 2007), and is particularly important for STEM persistence among URM students (Espinosa, 2011).
- *STEM intentions* reflect students' short- and long-term goals to pursue a STEM major, attend and complete graduate school in STEM, and establish a career in STEM. STEM intentions are associated with STEM persistence (Maltese & Tai, 2011; Shaw & Barbuti, 2010).

We prioritize STEM interventions that report objective outcome metrics of STEM performance, persistence, and success, three terms often used interchangeably in the STEM intervention literature, and operationalized as course grades, cumulative grade point averages (GPAs), yearly retention rates, graduation rates, graduate school admission, and career choices. Finally, we included STEM interventions that report a majority of URM, relative to non-URM, students as participants. The Women in Applied Science and Engineering Program (WISE) at Arizona State University (Newell, Fletcher, & Anderson-Rowland, 2002), for example, targets women, a group that is underrepresented, but it was not included because it did not target a majority of URM students nor did it report any social psychological variables. Finally, we excluded STEM interventions that did not fit within one of our four phases of social integration (e.g., graduate school or middle school interventions).

To identify papers with STEM interventions included in this Element, we entered keywords "STEM intervention," "STEM retention," "STEM recruitment," "STEM identity," "STEM persistence," "STEM summer bridge," and "STEM leaky pipeline" separately into Google scholar. Then we confirmed that the studies in these papers met our inclusion criteria. Finally, we searched through the papers' "cited-by" list to identify additional papers. Table 1 lists the STEM interventions included in this review.

It is important to note that the measures (qualitative vs. quantitative), definitions and types of STEM-related social psychological variables, and designs (cross-sectional vs. longitudinal; quasi-experimental vs. experimental) are inconsistently adopted across STEM interventions. We compare and contrast the different interventions across multiple STEM fields to synthesize findings into a coherent multiphase framework.

5 Phase 1: High School

High school institutions should integrate URM students into STEM communities during adolescence because early STEM identification and interest are robust predictors of future STEM performance (Chemers et al., 2011; Tai, Liu, Maltese, & Fan, 2006). Moreover, high school STEM preparation, SAT mathematics scores, and high school class rank are consistent predictors of STEM persistence (Alkhasawneh & Hargraves, 2014; Chang et al., 2014; Lee & Luyckx, 2006; Shaw & Barbuti, 2010; Wang, 2013). This integration phase coincides with a sensitive period in identity development among adolescents (Erikson, 1968). High school STEM interventions promote early opportunities to develop a STEM identity through content exposure and community.

Applied Social Psychology

Table 1 STEM interventions that meet inclusion criteria

Intervention Papers	Phase of Integration	Social Psychological Measure(s) Quantitative	Qualitative	Objective STEM Outcome Measure (s)	Cohort (s) Total Sample Size[a]
Bystydzienski, Eisenhart, & Bruning, 2015	1	Yes	Yes	Yes	131
Hernandez-Matias et al., 2019	1	Yes	Yes	No	25
Kuchynka, Reifsteck, Gates, & Rivera, 2020	1	Yes	No	No	77
Bruno et al., 2016	2	Yes	Yes	No	64
Graham, McIntee, Raigoza, Fazal, & Jakubowski, 2016	2	No	Yes	Yes	48
Liu, 2018	2	Yes	No	No	39
Pritchard, Perazzo, Holt, Fishback, McLaughlin, Bankston, & Glazer, 2016	2	Yes	Yes	Yes	26
Tomasko, Ridgway, Waller, & Olesik, 2016	2	Yes	Yes	Yes	188
Reyes, Anderson-Rowland, & McCartney, 1999	2	No	Yes	Yes	119
Gilmer, 2007	2, 3, 4	No	Yes	Yes	69

Table 1 (cont.)

Intervention Papers	Phase of Integration	Social Psychological Measure(s) Quantitative	Qualitative	Objective STEM Outcome Measure (s)	Cohort (s) Total Sample Size[a]
Maton et al., 2016	2, 3, 4	Yes	No	Yes	109
Kamangar, Silver, Hohmann, Mehravaran, & Sheikhattari, 2019	3, 4	Yes	No	No	46
Matsui, Liu, & Kane, 2003	3, 4	Yes	No	Yes	143
Estrada, Eppig, Flores, & Matsui, 2019	3, 4	Yes	No	Yes	68
Slovacek, Whittinghill, Tucker, Rath, Peterfreund, Kuehn, & Reinke, 2011	3, 4	Yes	No	Yes	198
Estrada, Hernandez, & Schultz, 2018	4	Yes	No	Yes	1420

[a] Sample sizes reflect the total number of participants included in the analyses from studies in intervention papers that met our inclusion criteria. The actual total number of participants in the intervention may be larger.

We acknowledge that students can start forming a STEM identity even prior to high school, which, in theory, results in even stronger and more stable STEM identities over time. However, we treat the high school experience as our initial phase because it marks the beginning of advanced and varied STEM course exposure and a choice to enroll in these courses. Before high school, students are automatically enrolled in science and math courses and thereby on a STEM trajectory by default. The high school phase reflects students' first opportunity to make class choices related to their future in STEM – indeed, completing advanced high school STEM classes is important for future college success (Tyson, Lee, Borman, & Hanson, 2007). Although Asian and White students take more STEM high school classes compared with their URM peers (Maltese & Tai, 2011), URM students who complete advanced STEM high school courses are as likely to complete STEM college degrees (Tyson et al., 2007). These findings indicate that under the right circumstances and given the right opportunities in high school, URM students fare just as well as non-URM students.

5.1 High School Programs

Though most interventions focus on URM STEM persistence during college or the summer prior to college (reviewed in Sections 6 to 8), the available research on Phase 1: High School elucidates the importance of promoting a STEM identity during middle adolescence (ages 14–17). To our knowledge, only three STEM high school interventions that target URM students meet our inclusion criteria (Bystydzienski, Eisenhart, & Bruning, 2015; Hernandez-Matias et al., 2019; Kuchynka et al., 2020). Collectively, they suggest that intervening in high school benefits STEM-related social psychological factors.

5.1.1 Initial Exploration in Breadth

At the start of Phase 1: High School, URM students will most likely have a weak or nonexistent STEM identity due to limited prior exposure to STEM material, opportunities, career guidance, and ingroup members (Witkow & Fuligni, 2011). Phase 1's identity developmental processes via *initial exploration in breadth* begin with exposure to STEM material and the guidance of mentors and teachers. Consistent with our conceptualization of identity development, most high school students are in a pre–commitment-making stage where they have not explored or committed to any STEM identities nor have they developed any STEM interests, both of which are antecedents to setting academic and career goals and intentions in STEM (Lent, Brown, & Hackett, 1994; Lent et al., 2016; Mangu, Lee, Middleton, & Nelson, 2015). Some research even indicates that developing an interest in STEM during high school is a stronger predictor of STEM persistence than high school STEM achievement (Maltese & Tai, 2011). However, students generally show a decline in STEM interest from elementary to secondary education (VanLeuvan, 2004; Wells et al., 2007), but this can be prevented and even reversed by interventions that expose students to varied

STEM material outside of traditional classroom settings (Young, Ortiz, & Young, 2017).

A four-week summer earth, environment, and engineering program, funded by NSF, examined the social psychological processes that promote a STEM identity and interest among URM high school students from Newark, New Jersey (Kuchynka et al., 2020). The program introduced students to earth science material through classroom settings, field trips, group projects, and exposure to early career STEM professionals who were guest speakers (most of whom were URM). Students interacted with URM and non-URM science teachers, URM undergraduate student mentors, and a diverse group of peers. Data were collected using validated psychological measurements at the start, middle, and end of the program. Relative to when they started the program, students demonstrated stronger STEM identities, general interest in STEM material, peer-to-peer relationships, undergraduate mentor–student relationships, and teacher-student relationships by the last day of the program. In addition, the type of relationship that promoted STEM identity among URM students was isolated by directly comparing the independent roles of relationship quality with peers and under-graduate mentors versus teachers. Of these three, only high-quality relationships with undergraduate mentors facilitated STEM identity over the course of the four-week program. Furthermore, subjective identification with the undergraduate mentors facilitated relationship quality, suggesting that similarities in age, race, ethnicity, socioeconomic status, and regional background promote high-quality mentor-student relationships that in turn strengthen STEM identity.

In another study, a three-year longitudinal intervention evaluated the impact of a high school program in which female students who were majority URM from low-income families and would-be first-generation college students par-ticipated in engineering projects and field trips and received college guidance on their interest in engineering (Bystydzienski et al., 2015). Professional engineers and staff members who were tasked with creating a micro-community where students felt encouraged to pursue engineering long term mentored female high school students. This program effectively combined assumptions of identity development by offering long-term exposure to engineering material in a range of formats, a diverse community of like-minded female-URM students, and a variety of mentorships from STEM group members. Participants, who com-pleted multiple measures repeatedly over three years, reported increases in engineering interest, content knowledge, and future goals to pursue engineer-ing. The intervention also tracked female URM participants through college (see Phase 4: College Second Year through Graduation).

In a third intervention, Hernandez-Matias et al. (2019) compared two one-week high-school programs with Puerto Rican students that focused on molecular biology and cancer research. Students in an experimentation group conducted hands-on experiments, while students in a non-experimentation group were exposed to science material (e.g., gene-editing models) but did not engage in hands-on experiments. Students in both groups were provided mentorship (science instructors) and participated in science laboratory tours. All students demonstrated increases in STEM identity strength, but this effect was stronger among students in the non-experimentation group. Students in the experimentation group exhibited smaller identity strength changes and reported more difficulties with learning content. Based on diaries and interviews, students in both groups reported that mentorship was a key component to their science identity development.

5.2 Discussion

The three interventions reviewed here (Bystydzienski et al., 2015; Hernandez-Matias et al., 2019; Kuchynka et al., 2020) provided an array of mentorship opportunities for URM students, while immersing them in a group of like-minded URM peers. The programs also provided opportunities for students to explore STEM material through active learning methodologies such as group projects and using instrumentation in a science laboratory. The interventions demonstrated increases in STEM identity strength and STEM interest.

Traditional classroom settings often evoke STEM stereotypes that threaten and alienate stigmatized students and undermine their STEM interest (Cheryan, Master, & Meltzoff, 2015; Cheryan, Meltzoff, & Kim, 2011; Cheryan, Plaut, Davies, & Steele, 2009; Master, Cheryan, & Meltzoff, 2016). High school interventions combat these issues by exposing students to STEM material across a variety of environments (field trips, laboratories) and incorporating active learning (group projects, conducting experiments) in more inclusive and diverse environments (Ballen, Wieman, Salehi, Searle, & Zamudio, 2017). Active learning components offered in nontraditional education settings are particularly beneficial because they close academic achievement gaps between URM and non-URM students through increased self-efficacy (Ballen et al., 2017) and stimulate URM high school students' interest and intent to pursue STEM careers (Gates & Kalczynski, 2016).

The findings from high school interventions also highlight the value of mentorship, particularly the mentorship high school students received from undergraduate college students. STEM mentors can offer guidance, impart knowledge, and teach expectations to high school students. According to the stereotype inoculation model (reviewed earlier; Dasgupta, 2011), subjective identification and perceived expertise in STEM are two mentor-related factors critical for inoculating URM students against negative stereotypes. Exposure to ingroup experts is most impactful when students subjectively identify (on race, ethnicity, age, gender, etc.) with the ingroup exemplars (Stout et al., 2011), which facilitates URM students' beliefs that they too can achieve future success in STEM (Morgenroth, Ryan, & Peters, 2015). Accordingly, undergraduate mentors may yield a stronger impact on STEM identity than STEM teachers because the former provide a more realistic upward comparison. Teachers are more of an established STEM expert than undergraduate students, but they may be too advanced in their career trajectory for high school students to easily imagine themselves following a similar path. Positive interactions with URM undergraduate mentors facilitate STEM identity because they have achieved admirable and attainable levels of STEM expertise and success. The overlapping identities of undergraduate and high school students presumably facilitate social bonding, familiarity, and accessibility resulting in high-quality relationships.

The findings from Hernandez-Matias et al. (2019), which compared two one-week high school interventions, suggest that the combination of mentorship and science material exposure is more meaningful for identity development than the combination of mentorship and hands-on experimentation. Since students in the experimentation group reported lower gains in STEM identity and more difficulties with the material, researchers and practitioners may need to consider the aptitude of high school students and not overwhelm them with tasks that are too advanced. Overwhelming challenges may have the opposite effect such that students may associate negative affect with STEM and believe they cannot perform adequately in STEM. In the end, such experiences and feelings may slow identity development.

Two of the high school interventions focused on exposing students to a single discipline (earth science in Kuchynka et al., 2020, and engineering in Bystydzienski et al., 2015). While exposure to a single STEM discipline can start the exploration process, a central component of exploration is the weighing of alternatives to evaluate one's options (Gati & Asher, 2001; Luckyx et al., 2006). High school students should have the opportunity to assess which STEM discipline most closely matches their interests, goals, and abilities through exposure to a variety of STEM areas. Exposure to a breadth of STEM disciplines is particularly important during high school because students are still pre–commitment making and thus need exposure to identify their interests.

There is limited research on high school STEM interventions with URM students, which presents an important gap in the empirical literature, and an underutilized potential solution to combat the loss of STEM interest observed among many high school students (Chen & Soldener, 2013; Rogers & Ford,

1997). It is well documented that pre-college characteristics (e.g., STEM preparation) are contributors to different graduation rates between URM and non-URM students (Alkhasawneh & Hargraves, 2014; Chang et al., 2014; Lee & Luyckx, 2006; Shaw & Barbuti, 2010; Pascarella & Terenzini, 1983; Wang, 2013), but the vast majority of STEM interventions target URM college (or pre-college summer) students once they have decided to pursue a STEM major (reviewed in Sections 6 to 8). High school interventions provide unique opportunities for young, undecided students prior to starting a STEM college education and career trajectory. These interventions provide early-on opportunities for initial exploration in breadth that promote strong STEM identities and interest through early exposure to varied STEM disciplines via novel nontraditional classrooms settings with active learning components.

6 Phase 2: Pre-College Summer

Though the summer before the start of college reflects a brief two- to three-month period, it is a discrete phase of STEM integration due to the critical transition from high school to college. The first two psychological stages of college integration are separation and transition (Tinto, 1988). For some students, college represents the first time they move away from their family and communities, which may pose challenges for students who rely on them for social support. During the separation period, students need to be inducted into a new social support system to begin a successful integration process (Tinto, 1988). For many students the transition to campus life may include the following changes: (a) physical – moving to the location of their college or university, (b) social – unfamiliar community and building new relationships, (c) psychological – shifting from a high school to a college identity and coping with self-doubt about abilities and belonging (Rosenthal, London, Levy, & Lobel, 2011), and/or (d) behavioral – new daily routine.

Because of the multiple types and sheer amount of changes, psychological adaption and potential distress is relatively steep in Phase 2: Pre-college Summer (and Phase 3: College First Year, discussed next). Incoming students can experience maladaptive enculturation that includes feelings related to losing identities and to isolation because of detachments from their familiar community and routines (Hurtado, Carter, & Spuler, 1996). The transition into college presents unique obstacles for students lower in socioeconomic status because they are more likely to perceive an incompatibility between their old and new academic identities (Iyer et al., 2009), an experience more likely to occur among URM students who tend to come from lower socioeconomic backgrounds and are first-generation when compared with non-URM students

(Allen-Ramdial & Campbell, 2014; Choy, 2001; McCarron & Inkelas, 2006). However, providing students with an academic environment that suits specific group-based needs promotes academic engagement (Eccles et al., 1993), and providing environments that facilitate perceptions of identity compatibility among marginalized group members eases the psychological distress experienced during academic transition periods (Rosenthal et al., 2011). Thus, identity development needs close attention during this fragile transition period through guidance, mentorship, and community. To that end, summer bridge programs support seamless transitions into college environments.

6.1 Summer Bridge Programs

Summer bridge programs are typically made up of daylong modules and activities that are aimed to increase content knowledge and feelings of preparedness (Ashley et al., 2017). Most summer bridge programs offer field trips, lectures from STEM professionals, self-reflection through journaling and group projects and may even provide the opportunity for students to complete coursework prior to the start of the first college semester (Ashley et al., 2017). These pre-college summer STEM experiences prepare students for challenging gateway courses (required introductory courses for a STEM major) during the first year of college. Summer bridge programs vary in length and content and in what each program measures and reports, but their general approach is to increase STEM interest and corresponding academic success to facilitate long-term retention efforts. To examine *continued exploration of breadth* during this period of social and academic transition, we first turn to summer bridge programs that target incoming URM students across a range of STEM disciplines. Then to evaluate *initial exploration in depth*, we review summer bridge programs that focus on only one STEM area.

6.1.1 Continued Exploration of Breadth

Because Phase 2 occurs prior to the start of first-year college classes, students will begin weighing potential STEM options via exposure to varied STEM disciplines across multiple contexts (e.g., lectures, laboratories, field settings). To illustrate the importance of continued exploration of breadth from Phase 1 to Phase 2, many STEM students enter college with the goal of becoming a medical doctor and are unaware or have little knowledge of STEM research careers. To address this issue, summer bridge programs teach students about a variety of STEM careers beyond medicine that may better suit their interests (Kuchynka, Findley-Van Nostrand, & Pollenz, 2019).

The AIMS summer bridge program at Bowling Green State University exposed incoming URM students to a variety of STEM course material such as biology, chemistry, and geology via lectures and laboratory settings (Gilmer, 2007). Such varied exposure is important for exploration of breadth because it allows students to learn from multiple STEM leaders, get hands-on experience with the content, and increase the frequency of interactions with STEM group members. In addition to acquiring STEM knowledge from college coursework, students participate in extracurricular nonacademic activities like cookouts to foster belonging to the STEM community. The intervention administered only qualitative measures, on which URM students described that the summer bridge program opened their eyes to science fields outside of medicine and that taking classes with other URM students in addition to the leisurely activities facilitated their sense of belonging.

HāKilo, a six-week summer bridge program in the University of Hawaii system, assisted URM community college students with the goal of transferring to four-year colleges (Bruno et al., 2016). Students took math courses each morning and were exposed to different STEM disciplines each afternoon. Also, students were offered career exploration services, participated in extracurricular activities with their cohort, and were assigned undergraduate student mentors who were returning students. Relative to the start of the program, quantitative posttest measures administered six weeks later revealed that students exhibited increased knowledge about potential STEM career options, greater self-efficacy, and stronger intentions to pursue a STEM major.

Another summer bridge program at a predominately White institution enrolled incoming URM STEM students in a six-week program where they completed math and physics courses (Liu, 2018). Students attended lecture-based courses to prepare them for the intensity they would encounter in college STEM coursework. Researchers quantitatively tracked changes in self-efficacy and math anxiety across the duration of the program. Interestingly, students' physics self-efficacy decreased over the course of the program and their math self-efficacy remained unchanged. However, students' math anxiety significantly decreased by the end of the summer program.

Finally, Ohio's Science and Self-Expansion Program (OSTEP) at Ohio State University recruited URM and first-generation students who expressed interest in STEM to participate in a six-week summer bridge program that encompassed exposure to all STEM disciplines (Tomasko, Ridgway, Waller, & Olesik, 2016). OSTEP provides extensive feedback on the expectations of campus life including a clear understanding of the STEM major workload, a STEM residence with a cohort that subsequently goes through college together, and socially supportive class structures. Relative to the start of the program, quantitative and qualitative data demonstrated that students had stronger feelings of preparedness and a sense of belonging at the end of the six-week program. Tracking student academic records showed that URM OSTEP students were also retained in STEM at higher levels than the general STEM student population.

6.1.2 Initial Exploration in Depth

For students entering college in pursuit of a specific STEM major, STEM-specific summer bridge programs can jumpstart *initial exploration in depth*. Because these students have begun the initial commitment making by intending to major in STEM before the start of their first college year, they can begin evaluating their commitment through more advanced content exposure and interactions with ingroup members. Three STEM-specific summer bridge programs that met our inclusion criteria examined initial exploration in depth.

First, the Future Chemists Scholarships and Support (FoCuS) program at both the College of Saint Benedict and Saint John's University in Minnesota targeted incoming URM students who sought to major in chemistry (Graham, McIntee, Raigoza, Fazal, & Jakubowski, 2016). The program provided career exploration options in chemistry and students completed their first chemistry course. FoCuS students' grades were higher than those of a matched comparison group that completed the chemistry course during the college year. The students' stronger performance presumably stems from a strong support system that included frequent interactions with faculty members, academic advising, and mentoring by an advanced undergraduate STEM student. Undergraduate student mentors provided extra tutoring and class support. A majority of students reported in interviews that an undergraduate student mentor was key to their success.

The Minority Engineering Program (MEP) at Arizona State University was designed to recruit more URM students to engineering and increase engineering retention (Reyes, Anderson-Rowland, & McCartney, 1999). Students who participated in the program were immersed in a diverse community of potential URM engineers, and advanced undergraduate engineering students served as mentors. One primary goal of the program was to prepare students for introductory engineering courses. Students were exposed to technical presentations and completed a team design project. The program aimed to develop students' abilities to work in teams and to better understand how to handle time pressures. URM students who participated in the program demonstrated stronger one-year university retention rates compared with those who did not participate. Students reported in focus groups that the team project experience was highly beneficial and learning about the expectations of the engineering major related to time pressures and course requirements helped prepare them for their courses.

Finally, the University of Cincinnati: Leadership 2.0 summer program targeted incoming URM nursing students (Pritchard et al., 2016). Students took

several science classes; lived with other nursing student peers; received financial support; were exposed to research laboratories; participated in community
outreach; engaged in extracurricular activities outside of academic settings,
such as visiting museums; and were assigned three advisors – a student affairs
academic advisor, a faculty advisor, and a full-time student resident advisor.
This study utilized quantitative and qualitative measures to evaluate students'
experiences and attitudes. First, over the program's six-week period, pre- to
posttest quantitative surveys revealed an increase in feelings of preparedness for
STEM coursework and that relationships with program peers and full-time
student resident advisors were the most important program components. In
addition, students reported in one-on-one interviews at the end of the program
that they felt a strong sense of community and connections to peers and faculty
members, and an increased passion for nursing. Finally, student performance
and retention tracked during the first year of college showed no differences in
course grades between URM student participants and the entire nursing student
population and higher grades than URM students who did not participate in the
program.

6.1.3 Initial Commitment Making

Phase 2: Pre-college Summer reflects a social and academic transition period
wherein URM students enter a new environment and begin the important
process of choosing courses, a college major, and what academic research
labs to join, which mark *initial commitment making*. This decision-making
period may seem overwhelming for incoming students; thus, summer bridge
programs can ease student anxiety by giving them extra time and guidance to
evaluate potential commitments that best suit their needs. By the time students
begin the first year of college, they typically start a singular STEM pathway
even though students have not officially declared a major. First-year college
students must decide on courses to fulfill a specific major, which leaves little
opportunity for exploration of alternative commitments. Summer bridge programs provide students with early STEM exposure through communicating
with peers, learning more domain-specific content knowledge, and guidance
from mentors (Bruno et al., 2016; Gilmer, 2007; Graham et al., 2016; Pritchard
et al., 2016; Reyes, Anderson-Rowland, & McCartney, 1999; Tomasko et al.,
2016).

6.2 Discussion

Three of the seven summer bridge programs reviewed earlier report relatively
superior first-year college grades among URM students (Graham et al., 2016;

Pritchard et al., 2016; Reyes, Anderson-Rowland, & McCartney, 1999). Strong course performance is important to STEM persistence (Alkhasawneh & Hargraves, 2014), feelings of competence, and overall identity development (Luyckx et al., 2009). This academic success is rooted in three common summer bridge program features that are likely synergistic: (1) a STEM community of diverse peers, (2) mentorship from advanced undergraduate students and faculty members, and (3) early exposure to STEM material that prepares them for first-year STEM coursework.

The successful transition from a high school to a college identity partly relies on the latter's compatibility with current identities (e.g., ethnic-racial identity) (Iyer et al., 2009). The sooner students begin identifying with a new social group, the sooner they start reaping the psychological and behavioral benefits provided by group membership (Greenaway, Amiot, Louis, & Bentley, 2017). New self-categorizations allow students to connect with others who share a common perspective and similar life goals (Ashforth & Mael, 1989). Therefore, group memberships provide stability, meaning, and social connection during transitions (Iyer, Jetten, & Tsivrikos, 2008). Summer bridge programs ease the transition from high school to college by immediately immersing incoming students into a community of like-minded peers with similar backgrounds that promotes a meaningful STEM identity. Being surrounded by diverse peers early on in the transition to college allows URMs to perceive identity compatibility between their ethnic-racial identities and their new STEM identity.

A noteworthy element of some summer bridge programs is providing students with nonacademic extracurricular activities (Bruno et al., 2016; Gilmer, 2007; Pritchard et al., 2016). These activities appear to strengthen social bonding with the STEM community, which is particularly important for URMs, especially female URMs, who tend to feel excluded by STEM peers and faculty (Foor, Walden, & Trytten, 2007; Ong, 2005). Importantly, a strong sense of belonging is tied to academic persistence and identity development (Hausmann, Schofield, & Woods, 2007; Tajfel, 1981; Tajfel & Turner, 1979, 1986). Thus, summer bridge programs that provide extra opportunities for social bonding beyond academic preparation are, at least in theory, important for forming and maintaining a strong STEM identity.

A consistent outcome of summer bridge programs is that students stress the importance of having an undergraduate peer mentor. Similar to the findings from Phase 1: High School, providing potential STEM students with an undergraduate mentor facilitates overlap in shared identities, social bonding, and the ability to envision their future selves experiencing success in STEM. URM mentors and peers counter negative subtle and overt messages about the STEM group prototype. Although prototypes reflect learned associations, they can be changed by short- and long-term exposure to varied group members (Fiske & Taylor, 1991), namely, successful URM individuals in STEM.

With respect to STEM self-efficacy, findings from summer bridge programs indicate that it sometimes increases (Bruno et al., 2016), but sometimes decreases (Liu, 2018). Summer bridge programs may adjust STEM expectations such that students may go into STEM programs with relatively high confidence about their abilities that then wanes after they are exposed to rigorous coursework and the time and effort required to succeed in STEM (Liu, 2018). Importantly, decreases in STEM self-efficacy from participating in summer bridge programs need not come at the expense of increased retention rates. Incoming students in the STEM Academy at the University of South Florida demonstrated decreases in self-efficacy after a one-week summer bridge program, but they demonstrated higher retention rates compared with a matched comparison group (Findley–Van Nostrand & Pollenz, 2017; Kuchynka et al., 2019). Notably, these findings were replicated across multiple cohorts, suggesting that lower self-efficacy reflects a clearer understanding of the level of ability required to succeed in STEM, which may better prepare incoming STEM students for challenging coursework.

Research that examines identity formation processes underlying career decisions emphasizes the importance of having students consider several suitable majors and career alternatives that should be explored in depth (e.g., Gati & Asher, 2001). Exploration is important because students need to go through a process of identity resolution to achieve a strong commitment to their final goals. Summer bridge programs that encompass all areas of STEM offer an opportunity to engage in the process of choosing among multiple possible STEM majors through exposure to a breadth of material. By comparison, summer bridge programs that target only one STEM discipline offer valuable exploration in depth but limit the scope of STEM opportunities.

The successful enactment of a group identity depends upon learning and adopting the corresponding group-based behaviors and beliefs (Eccles, 2009), and the development of an academic identity relies on perceptions of school support as measured by providing students with clear and consistent rules and group norms (Bizumic, Reynolds, & Meyers, 2012). Developing a STEM identity means that one adopts new behaviors (e.g., classroom etiquette and studying techniques), ways of thinking (e.g., problemsolving and new academic terminology), and motivations (e.g., interest in learning STEM material). Because URM students often lack social support in STEM contexts (Foor et al., 2007), summer bridge programs effectively ameliorate this issue by providing formal and informal academic and social support systems (Bruno et al., 2016; Gilmer, 2007; Graham et al., 2016; Pritchard et al., 2016; Reyes, Anderson-Rowland, & McCartney, 1999; Tomasko et al., 2016).

7 Phase 3: College First Year

Phase 3: College First Year centers on early STEM achievement because it is one of the most robust and consistent predictors of STEM persistence (Alkhasawneh & Hargraves, 2014; May & Chubin, 2003; Persaud & Freeman, 2005; Reason, 2003). STEM gateway courses, typically completed during the first year of college, often present a challenge for URM students due to the notoriously rigorous coursework (Fries-Britt et al., 2010; Gasiewski et al., 2012; Seymour & Hewitt, 1997). Because large lecture-style courses are more impersonal, students often struggle with engagement (Gasiewski et al., 2012; Johnson, 2007; Laboy, 2004). Moreover, URM students are more likely to experience an inhospitable STEM environment due to feelings of isolation and perceived racial bias (Hurtado, Newman, Tran, & Chang, 2010). Feelings of stress and anxiety associated with achieving academically during Phase 3 may be buffered by a strong STEM identity (Osbourne & Jones, 2011), which is a source of approach motivation or the impulse to work toward external goals (Harmon-Jones, Harmon-Jones, & Price, 2013). Strongly, compared with weakly, identified students faced with academic challenges and pressures put forth more effort instead of disengaging. Following the findings from Phases 1 and 2, STEM identity is enhanced through undergraduate peer mentorship during the first year of college. Undergraduate student mentors offer academic and social support that can ease stress and enhance academic performance (Phinney, Torres, Kallemeyn, & Kim, 2011).

7.1 Early-Stage Ongoing Academic Support Programs

First-year students are often challenged with feeling connected to a college community, adjusting to an unfamiliar environment with new norms, and the rigors of their first-year classes (Rosenthal et al., 2011). Early-stage ongoing academic support programs aid first-year students via mentorship, counseling, research opportunities, and living learning communities. They also provide similar services as Phase 2's summer bridge programs but with greater exploration in depth. Most ongoing academic support programs are broken into multiple parts for the duration of the students' undergraduate career. The number and length of the different parts vary among programs, but they generally consist of two to three distinct time periods with different services (Gilmer, 2007; Maton et al., 2016; Matsui, Liu, & Kane, 2003). In this section, we describe Phase 3's integration components of continued exploration in depth and continued commitment making, then examine them within the contexts of ongoing academic support programs and living learning communities.

7.1.1 Continued Exploration in Depth and Continued Commitment Making

Exploration in depth is an adaptive process conceptualized as an interest to continue gathering information with respect to one's commitments (Luyckx et al., 2006). Thus, proper internal (self-reflection) and external (information seeking and contact with other ingroup members) explorations are important for ensuing motivation to persist in domains that require high amounts of time and resources (Seymour & Hewitt, 1997). Furthermore, students need to match their personal interests, values, and abilities with an appropriate STEM major, and they should not feel forced to pursue commitments from external sources (e.g., family members, teachers) without thorough self-evaluation, as this may result in weak identification (Kaplan & Flum, 2010). Over time for URM STEM students, exploration in depth is positively associated with feelings of competence and negatively related to perceived effort costs of their major (drawbacks associated with time and effort; Perez, Cromley, & Kaplan, 2014). Early-stage ongoing academic support programs play an important role in these factors and processes related to exploration in depth and commitment making.

In the first- and second-year of the AIMS program at Bowling Green State University (Gilmer, 2007) reviewed earlier, students received ongoing once-a-week mentorship from a faculty member who was part of the summer bridge phase. AIMS students were also encouraged to get involved with undergraduate research. Students were provided continued breadth of STEM exposure via research meetings, presentations, conferences, and organizational club meetings. Through these activities, students can evaluate their STEM commitments by observing how well their interests and abilities align with research goals and future career options. Although a vast majority of AIMS students who majored in STEM did not pursue undergraduate research, they were still exposed to research opportunities through informal (research meetings) and formal (conferences) contexts. Students reported through testimonials that participation in research helped them feel like a scientist by being around other scientists. One participant even responded after joining a chemistry lab, "It's nice being around real scientists and doing chemistry. Now I know why I chose chemistry as my major." These self-reports indicate the importance of active participation in STEM.

Another academic support program is the Meyerhoff Scholars Program at the University of Maryland, Baltimore County (UMBC; Maton et al., 2016). This long-term retention program started with a summer bridge program and followed high-achieving URM students throughout college. Researchers investigated the mechanisms that promote STEM identity strength from the end of the summer bridge program through sophomore year. They found that over the course of this time period, perceived benefits of the program mediated the relation between sense of belonging and STEM identity (Maton et al., 2016). The perceived benefits measure inquired about financial aid, study groups, tutoring, academic advising, personal counseling from staff, mentoring and support, organized social activities, faculty involvement, interactions with UMBC administrators, the Meyerhoff community, and professional development. The Meyerhoff Scholars Program also demonstrated excellent objective outcomes such that, students were five times more likely to pursue STEM PhDs compared with similar students who did not participate in the program (Maton et al., 2012).

The Biology Scholars Program (BSP) at the University of California, Berkeley, was designed to increase the academic success and retention rates for URM students pursuing the biological sciences (Matsui, Liu, & Kane, 2003). In addition to receiving traditional elements of ongoing academic support programs like career services, research opportunities, advising, and mentorship, they were given resources to address personal and family issues. The URM students who participated in BSP graduated with higher GPAs than URM biology students not in BSP and had comparable GPAs to non-URM non-BSP students. Also, they graduated at higher rates than both URM and non-URM university students. These promising findings suggest that achievement gaps between URM and non-URM students can be closed, given the right circumstances and opportunities.

In a separate investigation of BSP, Estrada and colleagues (2019) examined longitudinal changes over the first year of college in BSP students' STEM identity, STEM self-efficacy, STEM values, and intentions to persist in STEM across four time points. Estrada et al. (2019) found no changes in these social psychological variables. They interpreted the stable levels as positive psychological indicators given that the first year of college marks a difficult transition period when URM STEM students are at a relatively high risk of attrition.

7.1.2 Living Learning Communities

Living learning communities (LLCs) are a notable example of an ongoing academic support program (Davis, John, Koch, Meadows, & Scott, 2010; Gilmer, 2007; Maton et al., 2012; Soldner, Rowan-Kenyon, Inkelas, Garvey, & Robbins, 2012). STEM-focused LLCs consist of residence halls for STEM students to live together in one location. These residential communities provide increased opportunities for mentorship and interactions with peers and STEM faculty. The 2007 National Study of Living-Learning Programs collected data on STEM- and non-STEM–focused LLCs across forty-six universities (Inkelas, 2008). Soldner et al. (2012) performed structural equation modeling on these data to examine STEM-focused psychological and academic outcomes between URM and non-URM students. Peers and faculty members influenced all students through two distinct pathways: academic support and social support. LLCs provided extra opportunities for academic conversations among peers, which consisted of study groups or discussions about content learned in classes. Academic peer conversations and course-related faculty interactions indirectly predicted STEM interest, college grades, and intentions to major in STEM. In addition, non-course-related faculty interactions predicted STEM interests. Thus, formal and informal interactions with faculty members and peers reflect an essential component of academic success. Furthermore, STEM students in LLCs were constantly surrounded by fellow STEM community members who offered emotional support, which indirectly predicted intentions to major in STEM.

7.2 Discussion

The first year of college represents a transitional period when students adjust to a new community and daily routine. Students who decide to pursue a STEM major start a process of academic and social integration that supports their developing STEM identity (Estrada et al., 2018; Kelman, 2006). Social identity development is, at least in part, a top-down process in which individuals learn from group leaders about the values, norms, and expectations consistent with a group identity (Postmes et al., 2006). When these beliefs are transmitted from STEM leaders to incoming students, they are maintained in a STEM community of peers. Interactions with peers results in two distinct pathways: active transmission through direct instructions and passive transmission by witnessing STEM ingroup members' behaviors.

LLCs support these pathways through formal and informal opportunities for exploration in depth. LLCs that offer STEM-central communities provide students an opportunity to negotiate their STEM identity with other ingroup members. According to the identity formation literature (e.g., Postmes et al., 2006), fellow ingroup members help students evaluate their STEM choices and determine the content of their STEM identity. Moreover, social identity theorists posit that individuals cannot fully identify with their ingroup without comparing them with an outgroup (Postmes et al., 2006). STEM students understand their group membership by differentiating themselves from non-STEM students. This process should be especially important for URM students who often feel excluded from STEM as a group and discipline. Thus, students may develop STEM ingroup favoritism during Phase 3: College First Year, which may contribute to feeling committed to their emerging identities.

The academic and social transitions of the first year of college are characterized by heightened stress stemming from uncertainty and lack of information (Schweiger & DeNisi, 1991), and students have yet to fully develop the necessary skills to succeed in their new environment (Robbins et al., 2006). Mentors can help alleviate stress during social identity transitions by teaching first-year students how to adjust to an unfamiliar environment (Phinney et al., 2011) and what norms and behaviors are needed to succeed in STEM. Undergraduate student mentors quell uncertainty concerns regarding belonging by providing social connections and friendship while imparting knowledge rooted in recent experiences related to classes, research, and campus life (Phinney et al., 2011). These lessons are particularly important for first-generation college students, a group that is more likely to include more URMs than non-URMs.

The findings from BSP (Estrada et al., 2019) indicate that URM students who participated in STEM interventions may not consistently demonstrate increases in STEM identity, self-efficacy, and intentions. Because the first year of college introduces students to difficult coursework among other transitional challenges such as separation from family and friends, student expectations are adjusted to reflect a more realistic understanding of the time, effort, and skills required for STEM success. Therefore, stable STEM identities and self-efficacy are not necessarily a failure of the STEM intervention – they reflect sustained pursuit of STEM goals in the face of a rigorous time of integration.

Two early-stage ongoing academic support programs were not mentioned earlier because they did not include measures of social psychological variables, but they do provide evidence of objective academic success. First, the University of Michigan STEM Academy (M-STEM) provided ongoing academic support to talented diverse engineering students during their first year of college (as well as the summer transition and sophomore year periods; Davis et al., 2010). URMs who participated in M-STEM had superior GPAs compared with engineering URMs who did not participate in the program. Second, the Program for Excellence in Education and Research in the Sciences (PEERS) at UCLA socializes URM students to the roles and expectations of the institution and their academic major through instruction and by immersion into a diverse STEM community (Toven-Lindsey, Levis-Fitzgerald, Barber, & Hasson, 2015). Relative to a matched comparison group, students in PEERS had higher grades in most gateway STEM courses and higher cumulative GPAs and persisted in a STEM major at higher rates.

Taken together, Phase 3: College First Year interventions and their components of mentorship, community, and research opportunities support success among URM students, thus addressing the achievement gaps between them and their non-URM student counterparts (Matsui, Liu, & Kane, 2003).

8 Phase 4: College Second Year through Graduation

Finally, Phase 4 represents the second year of college through graduation. The second year of college starts a transition period that marks a new phase of a student's college career (Hurtado, Carter, & Spuler, 1996). This phase is marked by far more choices, autonomy, and independence. Many students move off campus and leave their structured STEM communities (e.g., see the Michigan STEM academy; Davis et al., 2010); consequently, they lose much of the structured academic and social support these communities provide. Students also finish many required gateway courses resulting in more freedom to choose their classes. Last, most universities require students to declare a major during this phase leading to final commitment making, but this can be linked to either ruminative exploration or final exploration in depth. The ultimate goal of Phase 4 is for students to fully integrate, which is supported by late-stage ongoing academic support programs.

8.1 Late-Stage Ongoing Academic Support Programs

In Phase 4, students enjoy greater academic autonomy and choices and look ahead to post-graduation career plans. But with these exciting prospects comes the potential for experiencing ruminative exploration and its harmful psychological and mental health outcomes. Late-stage ongoing academic support programs and the guidance they provide aid students during Phase 4. Late-stage ongoing academic support programs tend to include the structure and content of Phase 3's early-stage academic support programs, in addition to support services such as graduate school exam preparation and advanced research opportunities such as senior thesis projects.

8.1.1 Ruminative Exploration

Ruminative exploration refers to a repetitive cycle of ruminative thoughts that results in feeling unable to control the current situation (Luyckx et al., 2008). Compared with exploration in depth, which is characterized by adaptive tendencies (e.g., curiosity, interest), ruminative exploration is characterized by maladaptive tendencies (e.g., depression, anxiety). Ruminative exploration is uniquely associated with lower levels of self-esteem and self-rumination, whereas exploration in depth is uniquely associated with self-reflection and unrelated to self-esteem (Luyckx et al., 2008). Relevant to STEM identity development, ruminative exploration may be associated with academic burn-out – feelings of emotional exhaustion and diminished accomplishment (Yang, 2004). Academic burnout can lead to reduced work motivation and higher dropout rates (Meier & Schmeck, 1985). While it is normal to experience some anxiety during developmental periods of identity exploration and identity achievement (Kaplan & Flum, 2010; Schwartz, 2001), academic support programs should include efforts to minimize or even thwart ruminative exploration and its psychological and mental health outcomes. These consequences can further manifest as lack of commitment to the university and loss of interest in STEM. Maintaining a STEM community through continued mentorship, research participation, and contact with fellow STEM peers may prevent ruminative exploration and its consequences during the final phase of integration. Moreover, a strong STEM identity can buffer STEM students from college stressors that result in poor academic performance and high dropout rates (Osborne & Jones, 2011; also see Finn, 1989).

8.1.2 Final Exploration in Depth and Final Commitment Making

Final commitment making occurs during Phase 4 because students declare a major(s), start forming future career plans, and often engage in original research. As such, final commitment making works in tandem with final exploration in depth, which is characterized by the evaluation of one's commitment to a specific STEM major. Exploration during Phase 4 is distinct from the earlier phases of integration because instead of weighing multiple identity options, students evaluate a single identity rooted in their STEM major. STEM identity development is an ongoing process of continuously revising and reevaluating group membership. URM students need to conclude that their STEM identity associated with their major closely aligns with their values, abilities, and personal interests. After a period of exploration via internal (self-reflection) and external (interacting with fellow scientists, participating in research, receiving mentorship) processes that start in Phase 1, students should feel satisfied with commitments made during Phase 4. Examining this single identity through various environments and experiences should result in a strong identification with STEM.

8.1.3 Full STEM Integration

Consistent with academic integration in general (Tinto, 1975, 1988), STEM integration reflects high levels of formal and informal STEM community participation. Phase 4 provides new formal participation opportunities like completing advanced college courses, being a member of research labs, and going to conferences, as well as ongoing informal participation opportunities like study groups. Formal and informal participation in STEM influences students' recurring exploration and evaluation of their commitment to STEM and their relationships with peers, mentors, and faculty. Moreover, both forms of participation ultimately help students achieve full STEM integration and a strong identification with STEM. Evidence for these relations come from reports on late-stage ongoing academic support programs.

In the AIMS program previously discussed (Gilmer, 2007), junior and senior students were also given graduate school entrance exam preparation to support their post-undergraduate STEM trajectory. Though retaining more students in the undergraduate STEM community is a primary goal of most ongoing academic support programs, post-undergraduate plans are essential for addressing the lack of qualified URM students going into graduate school and careers. URM students started planning and preparing for graduate school during Phase 4 through admission test workshops, career exploration services, and guidance from faculty mentors. In addition, upper-level students in Phase 4 presented talks to lower-level students about experiences ranging from STEM research to off-campus living. STEM talks benefit upper-level students through gaining presentation experience, but lower-level students also gain important identity development aspects through the transmission of ingroup experiences. AIMS scholars were retained at a 90 percent rate compared with 72 percent for a matched comparison group (Gilmer, 2007).

In the ASCEND program at Morgan State University, a primarily URM-serving institution, upper-level undergraduates participated in student-led research (Kamangar et al., 2019). ASCEND students experienced the entire research process including picking a topic, writing a proposal, and conducting research under the guidance of graduate students and faculty members. ASCEND also emphasized peer teamwork and group projects, which provided community and opportunities to learn from one another. Using quantitative measures, students were asked to report their current and retrospective beliefs from before they joined the program. Students reported increases in science identity strength, peer support, and self-efficacy. Students further reported in a qualitative assessment that ASCEND provided them with a welcoming community where they improved their social, research, and leadership skills.

Bystydzienski et al.'s (2015) high school engineering intervention described in Section 5 followed the mostly female URM students through college. Only 33 percent of the students pursued a STEM degree during college. Socioeconomic status predicted who pursued STEM during college; many of the URM female students did not have the financial resources to attend a college with an engineering program or even attend any college. Also, women who started college in pursuit of a STEM major and later switched to a non-STEM major reported on qualitative measures (face-to-face interviews, Facebook personal site postings, and direct messaging) that a lack of support from peers, faculty, and advisors was the key factor that drove them to change majors.

A large-scale longitudinal study of URM students across fifty universities surveyed junior and senior undergraduate students to examine post-graduation persistence (Estrada et al., 2018). Students were recruited from the US National Institutes of Health's Research Initiative for Scientific Enhancement (RISE) program and other similarly structured URM STEM interventions. URM students who participated in a STEM intervention were matched with comparable URM students who did not participate in an intervention. The study found that STEM identity was associated with long-term STEM persistence including choosing a STEM career post-graduation. The researchers further identified that quality mentorship and research experience predicted STEM career choice via STEM identity. The large and representative sample in a longitudinal study suggests that mentorship and research experience are definitive contributors to URM STEM identity and subsequent STEM persistence.

Finally, Slovacek et al. (2011) investigated the efficacy of the Minority Opportunities in Research (MORE) program at three large universities. MORE is an ongoing academic support program composed of financial aid, mentorship, STEM workshops, and a special emphasis on research opportunities. MORE URM students worked in research labs that provided opportunities to interact with faculty. The study identified specific aspects of the research experience that significantly predicted STEM persistence post-graduation – namely, conference presentations, mentorship from a faculty member, and faculty members' support for campus challenges outside of research. Presenting at research conferences highlights the value of active STEM participation, and it can also prepare students for the expectations of graduate school. Finally, faculty member support emphasizes the importance of academic as well as emotional support.

8.2 Discussion

The success of Phase 4 programs is linked to the robust and diverse academic and social support provided to students throughout the STEM integration process. Late-stage ongoing academic support programs provide promising rates of academic success by promoting a strong STEM identity. Ultimately, the high retention rates suggest that under the right circumstances, URM students can thrive in STEM.

The findings from Bystydzienski et al.'s (2015) engineering intervention that followed students from high school through college indicate that although fostering STEM interest in young adulthood is important for promoting future STEM intentions, barriers to STEM integration and success remain for female URM students. College STEM programs can be isolating for female URM students who face unique challenges related to their intersecting ethnic-racial and gender identities (Armstrong & Jovanovic, 2017). Thus, creating strong social support systems beyond high school is critical for addressing STEM pathways, especially for students with two (or more) identifications with marginalized groups that intersect (Espinosa, 2011).

Students start looking ahead to future career plans during Phase 4. Whether students intend to pursue graduate school or start a career post-college graduation, they benefit from academic support programs that provide career guidance and test preparation services. Two additional factors have been identified as contributors to post-graduation commitment. First, research experience is essential for the pursuit of a STEM career (Carter, Mandell, & Maton, 2009; Pender, Marcotte, Domingo, & Maton, 2010). Putting students in active research positions fosters feelings of achievement and belonging and further develops their STEM self-concept, compared with placing them in passive roles such as attending lecture-hall courses (Ballen et al., 2017). Conducting research places students on the side of knowledge creation instead of knowledge reception, which is meaningful for perceiving oneself as belonging to STEM and being recognized by fellow scientists and scientists-in-training. From social identity and self-categorization theoretical perspectives, participating in research provides more opportunities for group socialization. Contexts that provide regular contact with fellow STEM group members allow students to better understand shared characteristics and beliefs of STEM programs and facilitate a meaningful and coherent STEM identity and promote ingroup favoritism.

Second, the importance of taking on more leadership roles such as mentorship during Phase 4 is consistent with research on the protégé effect, which posits that students put forth more effort to learn material when they have to teach it to someone else (Chase, Chin, Oppezzo, & Schwartz, 2009). Beyond knowledge acquisition, some research even demonstrates that URM STEM mentors end up with superior grades when compared with other students in a STEM discipline (e.g., Gates, 2019). Therefore, there are objective (grades) and subjective (social psychological changes) benefits to advanced undergraduate students when they mentor lower-level STEM group members.

Finally, taking on mentorship and engaging in advanced active learning facilitate identity formation (Gilmer, 2007; Kamangar et al., 2019). Phase 4 students' transition from STEM mentee to STEM mentor signals greater integration into the STEM community. As STEM mentors, advanced URM students become the transmitters of appropriate ingroup norms and values to lower-level students. From the lower-level students' perspective, learning about STEM experiences from fellow URM STEM students prepares them for unforeseen challenges and navigation of campus life. Becoming a STEM mentor crystalizes URM students' role in STEM and transitions them from passively learning STEM material to actively becoming a fully integrated group member. Moreover, becoming a STEM mentor turns upper-level URM students into STEM prototypes for other incoming group members. As such, Phase 4 mentoring increases upper-level students' STEM identity centrality while increasing lower-level students' STEM identity typicality.

9 General Discussion

Social identity research emphasizes the importance of centrality (Tajfel & Turner, 1986), typicality (Leach et al., 2008; Starr, 2018; Wilson, & Leaper, 2016), and compatibility (Iyer et al., 2009) when URM students incorporate STEM into their self-concept. Coupled with the assumptions of developmental identity perspectives (Erikson, 1968; Luyckx et al., 2006, 2008), URM students need to be integrated into STEM starting in adolescence and through adulthood to feel like a fully committed STEM group member and to achieve a strong STEM identity. This Element organizes these STEM integration and identity processes for URM students into four phases. Phase 1: High School highlights initial exploration in breadth; Phase 2: Pre-college Summer consists of continued exploration in breadth, initial exploration in depth, and initial commitment making; Phase 3: College First Year involves continued exploration in depth and continued commitment making; and Phase 4: College Second Year through Graduation reflects ruminative exploration (and its prevention), final exploration in depth, final commitment making, and full integration in STEM. We reviewed fifteen STEM interventions that provided empirical support for these four phases, most importantly highlighting the themes of URM students' integration into STEM, and the development of their STEM identity and its relation to STEM success. Furthermore, two major common factors of STEM interventions were observed across all phases – mentorship and a community of like-minded peers. Next we reflect on the major themes of our review and then provide an analysis of the limitations and future directions of the state of STEM intervention research.

9.1 Exploration and Commitment Making

Since STEM identity development is an iterative process of exploration and commitment making, students should thoroughly assess their options from high school through college. The importance of providing students early and broad exposure to STEM material is demonstrated in the success of STEM interventions during Phase 1 and Phase 2. Before URM students can fully integrate into and identify with STEM, their interests need to be sparked through exploration and commitment making. Stimulating then maintaining STEM interest is an important first step in developing a strong STEM identity (Lent et al., 1994). Students should not feel tied to a commitment because of external sources such as parents pushing them to pursue STEM, as this will result in a weak STEM identity (Kelman, 2006). The process of exploration formally starts in high school, a low-stakes time period when they are pre–commitment making. A lack of early exposure to STEM in high school represents one reason students shy away from STEM or believe that becoming a medical doctor is the only STEM career option. To formulate academic and professional goals, students need to thoroughly examine their interests as early as possible. Similarly, only being exposed to STEM material in traditional classroom settings is often not stimulating enough for students to foster STEM interest and intentions.

Exploration looks different during each phase. While exploration may start as simply learning the content of different STEM areas, exploration with each phase should incorporate active research participation, conferences, and presentations. STEM interventions highlight the value of exploring material through active learning such as group projects, field trips, and involvement in research laboratories. To fully identify with STEM, students need to do science as an integrated STEM community member and not just as a student in STEM coursework. Receiving information in a classroom is passive and may feel impersonal due to large lecture-style courses. However, working in a research laboratory provides opportunities to interact with scientists and other scientists-in-training in close interpersonal professional settings. Experiences with STEM outside the classroom may help students engage with STEM material in more novel and exciting ways. Therefore, exploration should start broad during earlier phases then narrow in depth as students integrate in STEM.

When students are in college and commit to a major, they benefit from continued exploration in depth by gathering information and weighing alternatives with respect to their commitments. The resolution of conflicting interests is valuable in the context of STEM commitments because it reduces dissonance that can arise from feeling forced into a given major and not knowing if their interests may be better suited for another career. Thus, exploration and commitment making represent a cyclical process that continuously shapes one's STEM identity.

Though high-quality education and training during high school and college are essential for developing STEM identities, barriers remain for URM students post–college graduation in graduate school and their professional careers. Some reports demonstrate that the greatest disproportionate loss of URMs compared with non-URMs occurs during the transition from undergraduate to graduate programs (e.g., Allen-Ramdial & Cambell, 2014). Effective late-stage ongoing academic support programs prepare students for the rigors of graduate school and/or the STEM workforce by teaching the expectations, norms, and standards for the multiple stages across the STEM pathway. To provide a smooth, psychologically adaptive transition from undergraduate to graduate programs, students must strongly identify with STEM, hold high self-efficacy, and be committed to future goals in STEM. These factors also impact the transition into a career in STEM.

9.2 Changing the STEM Prototype

A pervasive concern for URMs entering and staying in STEM is the perceived incompatibility between their ethnic-racial identities and their STEM identities due to cultural stereotypes about who does and does not belong in STEM (Beasley & Fischer, 2012; Kellow & Jones, 2008). In response to negative cultural stereotypes, stigmatized group members make the stigmatized domain less central to their self-concept (Major et al. 1998). One way to combat the perceived lack of fit in STEM is by diversifying the STEM prototype of White or Asian men (Dasgupta, 2011; Stout et al., 2011). The more URMs are in contact with diverse STEM ingroup members, the more accessible a diverse STEM prototype, which, in turn, promotes perceived compatibility of URM students' ethnic-racial identity with their emerging STEM identity. Mentors and peers from URM groups can promote diverse STEM prototypes and their subsequent benefits.

9.2.1 Mentorship

This Element highlights the importance of providing students with an array of mentors but also demonstrates the unique influential role of advanced undergraduate students as peer mentors. In Phases 1–3 of integration, lower-level URM students benefit from witnessing and learning from someone with a similar background who is successful in STEM. Providing URM students a mentor with overlapping identities facilitates four psychological processes: (1) the transmission of STEM ingroup norms, (2) the ability to realistically imagine their future selves achieving a STEM degree and setting STEM career goals, (3) countering cultural stereotypes about who belongs in STEM, and (4) learning how to navigate campus climates that may sometimes be isolating.

The quality of mentorship – frequent warm and positive relationship interactions – moderates STEM identity development (Kuchynka et al., 2020). In these relationships, advanced undergraduate students serve as near-peer mentors, who, as discussed earlier, are mentors slightly more advanced in their academic trajectory who advise and support high school students, summer bridge students, and first-year undergraduate students. Accordingly, the overlapping identities between near-peer mentors and mentees should promote social bonding, familiarity, and accessibility. The STEM interventions reviewed throughout this Element highlight the importance of near-peer mentors across each integration phase (Phase 1: Kuchynka et al., 2020; Phase 2: Bruno et al., 2016; Graham et al., 2016; Pritchard et al., 2016; Reyes, Anderson-Rowland, & McCartney, 1999; Phase 3: Gilmer, 2007; Phase 4: Kamangar et al., 2019). Of particular interest is the potential scalability of near-peer mentors across high schools and college campuses. Given the dearth of URM STEM faculty members, undergraduate upper-level STEM students are a large, untapped population of potential URM mentors in academic settings.

URM STEM students who enter Phase 4 continue to be mentees but become mentors as well. More specifically, they receive mentorship from faculty members or graduate students, but they also reach the point in integration where they become the transmitter of ingroup values, norms, and behaviors they started learning in the early phases of STEM integration. Moreover, being a mentor has dual benefits – it can increase the centrality of STEM into upper-level students' self-concept and increase lower-level students' perceived typicality of URM STEM group members.

9.2.2 Community of STEM Peers

Belonging to a community is particularly important for URM students in STEM (Strayhorn, 2011), but this connection may be difficult to initiate and maintain when URM students are in predominantly White higher education institutions in addition to disciplines that are overly represented by White and Asian men. With a focus largely on testing and grades in academic settings, feelings of relatedness and belonging are often ignored as important contributors to academic success. Students need close relationships with like-minded peers and mentors to gain access to valued resources such as knowledge, research opportunities, tutoring, and guidance on career paths, which all influence STEM identity. Notably, interventions find that feelings of belongingness with a STEM community facilitate both STEM identity (Kuchynka, Findley-Van Nostrand, & Pollenz, 2019) and STEM success (Mondisa & McComb, 2015).

9.3 Limitations and Future Directions

The STEM interventions reviewed here provide excellent empirically based resources for institutions that wish to promote and improve the STEM academic and professional success of their URM students. However, STEM intervention science is relatively new and, like most novel research, it includes limitations that need to be addressed in future research.

9.3.1 Methodological Approaches

Some STEM interventions only adopted qualitative methods such as interviews and focus groups (Gilmer, 2007; Reyes, Anderson-Rowland, & McCartney, 1999). Qualitative methods offer valuable insights into student experiences, such as spontaneous thoughts on and feelings about the valuable components of a STEM intervention and suggestions for ways to improve programs. Interviews and focus groups offer nuanced and comprehensive descriptions of students' experiences often obscured with the sole use of quantitative methods. Thus, qualitative methods offer a unique opportunity for researchers to explore mechanisms for student success.

However, STEM intervention researchers should also include quantitative methods to determine what psychological factors and processes predict academic success. Their absence in STEM intervention research prevents researchers from isolating the relatively strong and consistent factors and mechanisms that strengthen (or weaken) STEM identity throughout integration. Furthermore, quantitative methods allow for meta-analyses, which could identify the most impactful components across multiple STEM interventions. Finally, researchers need to report effect sizes because they provide the magnitude of an intervention's influence and allow researchers to compare findings across different interventions.

We also urge researchers to adopt quantitative methods because they allow for advanced statistical modeling that tests for the factors and mechanisms underlying positive changes in STEM interventions. This will permit researchers to more definitively understand what contributes to STEM identity development and its corresponding academic and professional success in STEM. To illustrate, tracking changes in psychological variables over time (typically in a pre/posttest design) should be a benchmark to understanding the causal effects of STEM interventions. Furthermore, indirect effect models can address questions such as what programmatic elements underlie increases in STEM identity and other social psychological variables. The handful of researchers who have started this process demonstrate the consistent and important roles of feelings of belongingness and mentorship in STEM identity (e.g., Estrada et al., 2018; Inkelas, 2008; Kuchynka et al., 2019; Kuchynka et al., 2020; Maton et al., 2016).

9.3.2 Measuring Social Psychological Mechanisms

STEM interventions should regularly measure social psychological mechanisms such as STEM identity and STEM interest because they are key to understanding success. The wide variability in what STEM interventions measure and report makes it difficult to compare STEM identity and integration across interventions. Though there are many published reports on STEM interventions, only a small subset met our inclusion criterion of measuring social psychological variables. Perhaps a standardized set of validated measures could be used across interventions. For example, to receive funding, the National Science Foundation could require researchers to include these measures (in addition to researchers' measures of interest) in their STEM interventions. Our review suggests that researchers should measure STEM identity, interest, self-efficacy, belonging, and future STEM intentions across two or more time points. Due to the lack of consistency across measurements, the mechanisms underlying some of the effects reported in this review are speculative. Measuring social psychological variables and including them in quantitative models would reveal important mechanisms that drive STEM academic and professional success.

9.3.3 Experiences with Bias

Much of the research on URM students in STEM suggests that a primary issue is experience with overt and subtle forms of bias, which can cause URM students to feel isolated and as if they do not belong in STEM (Grossman & Porche, 2014). However, to our knowledge, experiences with ethnic-racial bias or perceptions of an inhospitable STEM context have not been measured in URM STEM interventions. Overt forms of ethnic-racial bias reflect hostile and antagonistic manifestations (e.g., harassment, group-based exclusion), whereas subtle forms are ambiguous and often go unnoticed but are experienced more frequently (e.g., avoidance, cold verbal or nonverbal cues) (Deitch, Barsky, Butz, Chan, Brief, & Bradley, 2003). Both types of bias may have unique consequences for URM student outcomes. For example, subtle, compared with overt, forms of gender bias in STEM are associated with poorer academic outcomes for women with weak STEM identities (Kuchynka et al., 2018). Future research should test these findings in the context of URM STEM student outcomes. Tracking URM students' experiences with bias will allow researchers to better understand the types of negative experiences URMs face over time and what programmatic elements best combat these experiences.

9.3.4 Implicit versus Explicit Beliefs and Attitudes

STEM intervention researchers almost exclusively rely on self-report measures of beliefs and attitudes. These measures are valuable for tracking experiences related to explicit beliefs and attitudes stemming from conscious awareness and controlled cognitive processes (Gawronski & Payne, 2011; Greenwald & Banaji, 1995). However, researchers should also incorporate measures of implicit attitudes and beliefs – that is, mental associations that are automatic and that operate outside of the conscious awareness. According to Dasgupta et al.'s (2011) stereotype inoculation model, subtle cues about STEM belongingness may not be represented in URM students' conscious awareness. Such cues can be transmitted by observing the disproportionate ratios of URM to non-URM students in STEM courses. These cues about belonging have a stronger impact on implicit, compared with explicit, self-stereotyping (Stout et al., 2011). Since URM students receive subtle messages about STEM stereotypes, the impact of exposure to ingroup role models or mentors on URM students' self-concept may be observed on measures of implicit attitudes and beliefs. Only measuring URM students' explicit attitudes and beliefs may miss important aspects of STEM integration and identity.

9.3.5 Implementing Lessons from STEM Interventions

As discussed in the Introduction, many research efforts have been implemented over the past three decades to improve URM representation in STEM in the United States, but they have yet to achieve parity (National Science Foundation, 2019). One reason might be that any gains observed are limited to STEM interventions. STEM interventions are effective at increasing URM STEM academic and professional success (Ashley et al., 2017; Estrada et al., 2018), but URM students outside interventions continue to face barriers in STEM, resulting in the sustained loss of potential talent. The lessons from STEM interventions need to be applied to high schools and college campuses that seek to improve URM STEM retention.

Inspired by lessons learned from past interventions, the present authors are currently engaged in a series of cutting-edge intervention and research studies that focus on URM STEM identity and persistence. Funded by the National Science Foundation, the Louis Stokes Alliance for Minority Participation (LSAMP) program is a multi-college alliance-based program aimed at increasing URM student recruitment and retention in STEM across the United States (Clewell, 2006). LSAMP programs provide ongoing academic support for participants throughout college and, in some cases, graduate school. Students receive academic support, research funding, research opportunities, and mentorship from undergraduate student peers and faculty members, and they participate in a diverse community of LSAMP peers. We are investigating LSAMP URM students' experiences but also untangling the most impactful elements of this far-reaching STEM retention program. Quantitative techniques are being applied to understand what type of mentorship (undergraduate students, staff, and faculty) promotes positive psychological processes and STEM outcomes. We are measuring implicit and explicit attitudes and beliefs as well as investigating URM students' experiences with bias in STEM. One goal is to understand how experiences with bias influence URM identity development and the psychological mechanisms that buffer such experiences.

Also, we are adopting experimental designs to test recruitment strategies targeting URM students and their effect on STEM interest. URM students in STEM will also be longitudinally tracked over time to evaluate their STEM identity formation through Phase 3: College First Year and Phase 4: College Second Year through Graduation. Finally, we are using advanced statistical models to test the underlying mechanisms that strengthen versus weaken STEM identity across time, such as motivations, mentorship, belonging to a diverse community, self-efficacy, and experiences with bias. This program of ongoing and future research will inform both STEM science researchers and higher education leaders and faculty about the programmatic and psychological elements most strongly linked to STEM academic success among URM students.

9.4 Implications

This Element focuses on the STEM experiences and success of URMs in the United States because of the country's historic systems of stratification that created unequal educational and career access and opportunities for URM populations (National Science Board, 2015). However, other countries have a need for effective STEM recruitment and greater access to high-quality education and training among their student populations (Schwab & Sala-i-Martín, 2012). We suspect that many of the basic assumptions underlying the findings reviewed in this Element generalize broadly. Though other countries do not have the same educational time periods as the United States (e.g., a three-month summer break before college), the basic principles of the iterative exploration and commitment process still apply. In general, students need varied and novel exposure to STEM material during adolescence, which should be shifted to more focused and active exploration and commitment during college. Similarly, the efficacy of peer mentors and diverse STEM communities should be just as important in other countries, especially those with diverse URM groups.

Although URMs face structural disadvantages that result in unique barriers in STEM, many of the intervention components described in this Element are important to non-URM student success as well. Connections to others via mentorship relationships and a welcoming community of peers are essential components of integration for all students (Tinto, 1975, 1988). However, these needs are heightened for URMs because they are more likely to experience belonging uncertainty in STEM and they face negative cultural stereotypes and discrimination in STEM (Walton & Cohen, 2007, 2011).

9.5 Conclusion

In the United States, Black, Latinx, and Native American students remain underrepresented across STEM disciplines, in large part because of ethnic and racial biases in STEM and because URMs often lack adequate resources, access to quality training, and ample opportunities (National Science Board, 2015). STEM interventions can address these issues. When they establish the right circumstances, URM students persist in STEM at the same rate as non-URM students. Although this Element focuses on STEM identity development through participation in STEM interventions from high school to college, its findings can be applied to identity development more generally. STEM interventions often provide a controlled environment to evaluate dimensions of identity development, allowing researchers to infer the mechanisms underlying URM STEM success. The interventions in this review emphasize the importance of STEM exploration and commitment, mentorship, and community. Institutions should consider integrating the lessons from STEM interventions to all relevant programs in high schools, colleges, and universities, if they wish to promote and maintain STEM success among their URM students.

References

Alkhasawneh, R., & Hargraves, R. H. (2014). Developing a hybrid model to predict student first year retention in STEM disciplines using machine learning techniques. *Journal of STEM Education: Innovations and Research, 15*(3), 35–42.

Allen, T. D., Eby, L. T., & Lentz, E. (2006). Mentorship behaviors and mentorship quality associated with formal mentoring programs: Closing the gap between research and practice. *Journal of Applied Psychology, 91*(3), 567–578.

Allen-Ramdial, S. A. A., & Campbell, A. G. (2014). Reimagining the pipeline: Advancing STEM diversity, persistence, and success. *BioScience, 64*(7), 612–618.

American Institutes for Research. (2009) *The road to the STEM professoriate for underrepresented minorities: A review of the literature.* Washington, DC: American Institutes for Research.

Anderson, E., and Kim, D. (2006). *Increasing the success of minority students in science and technology.* Washington, DC: American Council on Education.

Andersen, L., & Ward, T. J. (2014). Expectancy-value models for the STEM persistence plans of ninth-grade, high-ability students: A comparison between Black, Hispanic, and White students. *Science Education, 98*(2), 216–242.

Armstrong, M. A., & Jovanovic, J. (2017). The intersectional matrix: Rethinking institutional change for URM women in STEM. *Journal of Diversity in Higher Education, 10*(3), 216–231.

Asgari, S., Dasgupta, N., & Cote, N. G. (2010). When does contact with successful ingroup members change self-stereotypes? A longitudinal study comparing the effect of quantity vs. quality of contact with successful individuals. *Social Psychology, 41*(3), 203–211.

Ashforth, B. E., & Mael, F. (1989). Social identity theory and the organization. *Academy of Management Review, 14*(1), 20–39.

Ashley, M., Cooper, K. M., Cala, J. M., & Brownell, S. E. (2017). Building better bridges into STEM: A synthesis of 25 years of literature on STEM summer bridge programs. *CBE Life Sciences Education, 16*(4), es3.

Atherton, M. C. (2014). Academic preparedness of first-generation college students: Different perspectives. *Journal of College Student Development, 55*(8), 824–829.

Ballen, C. J., Wieman, C., Salehi, S., Searle, J. B., & Zamudio, K. R. (2017). Enhancing diversity in undergraduate science: Self-efficacy drives performance gains with active learning. *CBE – Life Sciences Education, 16* (4), 56.

Bandura, A. (1986). The explanatory and predictive scope of self-efficacy theory. *Journal of Social and Clinical Psychology, 4*(3), 359–373.

Baumeister, R. F., & Leary, M. R. (1995). The need to belong: Desire for interpersonal attachments as a fundamental human motivation. *Psychological Bulletin, 117*(3), 497–529.

Beasley, M. A., & Fischer, M. J. (2012). Why they leave: The impact of stereotype threat on the attrition of women and minorities from science, math and engineering majors. *Social Psychology of Education, 15*(4), 427–448.

Berryman, S. E. (1983). *Who will do science? Trends, and their causes in minority and female representation among holders of advanced degrees in science and mathematics.* New York: Rockefeller Foundation.

Bhattacharya, B., & Hansen, D. E. (2015). Implementing a summer STEM bridge program. *Peer Review, 17*(2), 19–20.

Bizumic, B., Reynolds, K. J., & Meyers, B. (2012). Predicting social identification over time: The role of group and personality factors. *Personality and Individual Differences, 53*(4), 453–458.

Bodenhausen, G. V. (2010). Diversity in the person, diversity in the group: Challenges of identity complexity for social perception and social interaction. *European Journal of Social Psychology, 40*(1), 1–16.

Bonous-Hammarth, M. (2000). Value congruence and organizational climates for undergraduate persistence. In J. Smart, J. & W. Tierney, W. G. (Eds.), *Higher Education: Handbook of Theory and Research* (pp. 339–370). New York Agathon Press.

Braddock, J. H., & McPartland, J. M. (1987). How minorities continue to be excluded from equal employment opportunities: Research on labor market and institutional barriers. *Journal of Social Issues, 43*(1), 5–39.

Braxton, J. M. (1999). Theory elaboration and research and development: Toward a fuller understanding of college student retention. *Journal of College Student Retention: Research, Theory & Practice, 1*(2), 93–97.

Brewer, M. B. (1991). The social self: On being the same and different at the same time. *Personality and Social Psychology Bulletin, 17*(5), 475–482.

(1999). The psychology of prejudice: Ingroup love and outgroup hate? *Journal of Social Issues, 55*(3), 429–444.

Brown, B. A., Henderson, J. B., Gray, S., Donovan, B., Sullivan, S., Patterson, A., & Waggstaff, W. (2016). From description to explanation: An empirical exploration of the African-American pipeline problem in STEM. *Journal of Research in Science Teaching*, *53*(1), 146–177.

Bruno, B. C., Wren, J. L., Noa, K., Wood-Charlson, E. M., Ayau, J., Soon, S. L., Needham, H., & Choy, C. A. (2016). Summer bridge program establishes nascent pipeline to expand and diversify Hawaii's undergraduate geo-science enrollment. *Oceanography*, *29*(2), 286–292.

Byars-Winston, A. M., Branchaw, J., Pfund, C., Leverett, P., & Newton, J. (2015). Culturally diverse undergraduate researchers' academic outcomes and perceptions of their research mentoring relationships. *International Journal of Science Education*, *37*(15), 2533–2554.

Byars-Winston, A., Estrada, Y., Howard, C., Davis, D., & Zalapa, J. (2010). Influence of social cognitive and ethnic variables on academic goals of underrepresented students in science and engineering: A multiple-groups analysis. *Journal of Counseling Psychology*, *57*(2), 205–218.

Byars-Winston, A., Gutierrez, B., Topp, S., & Carnes, M. (2011). Integrating theory and practice to increase scientific workforce diversity: A framework for career development in graduate research training. *CBE Life Sciences Education*, *10*, 357–367.

Bystydzienski, J. M., Eisenhart, M., & Bruning, M. (2015). High school is not too late: Developing girls' interest and engagement in engineering careers. *The Career Development Quarterly*, *63*(1), 88–95.

Carlone, H. B., & Johnson, A. (2007). Understanding the science experiences of successful women of color: Science identity as an analytic lens. *Journal of Research in Science Teaching: The Official Journal of the National Association for Research in Science Teaching*, *44*(8), 1187–1218.

Carter, F. D., Mandell, M., & Maton, K. I. (2009). The influence of on-campus, academic year undergraduate research on STEM Ph. D. outcomes: Evidence from the Meyerhoff Scholarship Program. *Educational Evaluation and Policy Analysis*, *31*(4), 441–462.

Chang, M. J., Eagan, M. K., Lin, M. H., & Hurtado, S. (2011). Considering the impact of racial stigmas and science identity: Persistence among biomed-ical and behavioral science aspirants. *The Journal of Higher Education*, *82* (5), 564–596.

Chang, M. J., Sharkness, J., Hurtado, S., & Newman, C. B. (2014). What matters in college for retaining aspiring scientists and engineers from underrepresented racial groups. *Journal of Research in Science Teaching*, *51*(5), 555–580.

Chase, C. C., Chin, D. B., Oppezzo, M. A., & Schwartz, D. L. (2009). Teachable agents and the protégé effect: Increasing the effort towards learning. *Journal of Science Education and Technology*, *18*(4), 334–352.

Chemers, M. M., Zurbriggen, E. L., Syed, M., Goza, B. K., & Bearman, S. (2011). The role of efficacy and identity in science career commitment among underrepresented minority students. *Journal of Social Issues*, *67*(3), 469–491.

Chen, S., Binning, K. R., Manke, K. J., Brady, S., McGreevy, E. M., Betancur, L., Limeri, L. B., & Kaufmann, N. (2020). Am I a Science Person? A Strong Science Identity Bolsters Minority Students' Sense of Belonging and Performance in College. *Personality and Social Psychology Bulletin*.

Chen X., & Soldner, M. (2013). *STEM attrition: College students' paths into and out of STEM fields*. Washington, DC: U.S Department of Education, IES National Center for Education Studies.

Cheryan, S., Master, A., & Meltzoff, A. N. (2015). Cultural stereotypes as gatekeepers: Increasing girls' interest in computer science and engineering by diversifying stereotypes. *Frontiers in Psychology*, *6*, 49.

Cheryan, S., Meltzoff, A. N., & Kim, S. (2011). Classrooms matter: The design of virtual classrooms influences gender disparities in computer science classes. *Computers & Education*, *57*(2), 1825–1835.

Cheryan, S., Plaut, V. C., Davies, P. G., & Steele, C. M. (2009). Ambient belonging: How stereotypical cues impact gender participation in computer science. *Journal of Personality and Social Psychology*, *97*(6), 1045–1065.

Choy, S. (2001). Essay: Students whose parents did not go to college: Postsecondary access, persistence, and attainment. In J. Wirt, et al. (Eds.), *The condition of education 2001* (pp. XVIII–XLIII). Washington, DC: National Center for Education Statistics, U.S. Government Printing Office.

Chubin D. E., & DePass A. L. (2012). *Understanding Interventions That Broaden Participation in Research Careers: Intervening to Critical Mass*, vol. 5, Washington, DC: American Association for the Advancement of Science.

Clewell, B. C., De Cohen, C. C., Tsui, L., Forcier, L., Gao, E., Young, N., Deterding, N., & West, C. (2006). *Final report on the evaluation of the National Science Foundation Louis Stokes Alliances for Minority Participation Program*. Washington, DC: Program for Evaluation and Equity Research (PEER), The Urban Institute.

Crocker, J., & Schwartz, I. (1985). Prejudice and ingroup favoritism in a minimal intergroup situation: Effects of self-esteem. *Personality and Social Psychology Bulletin*, *11*(4), 379–386.

Dasgupta, N. (2011). Ingroup experts and peers as social vaccines who inoculate the self-concept: The stereotype inoculation model. *Psychological Inquiry*, *22*(4), 231–246.

Dasgupta, N., & Stout, J. G. (2014). Girls and women in science, technology, engineering, and mathematics: STEMing the tide and broadening participation in STEM careers. *Policy Insights from the Behavioral and Brain Sciences, 1*(1), 21–29.

Davidson, C., & Wilson, K. (2013). Reassessing Tint's concepts of social and academic integration in student retention. *Journal of College Student Retention: Research, Theory & Practice, 15*(3), 329–346.

Davis, C. S., St. John, E., Koch, D., & Meadows, G. (2010). Making academic progress: The University of Michigan STEM academy. Proceedings of the joint WEPAN/NAMEPA Conference, Baltimore, Maryland.

Deaux, K. (1994). Social identity. In E.T. Higgins & A.W. Kruglenski (Eds.), *Social Psychology. Handbook of Basic Principles.* (pp. 1–9). New York: The Guildford Press.

Deitch, E. A., Barsky, A., Butz, R. M., Chan, S., Brief, A. P., & Bradley, J. C. (2003). Subtle yet significant: The existence and impact of everyday racial discrimination in the workplace. *Human Relations, 56*(11), 1299–1324.

Dennehy, T. C., & Dasgupta, N. (2017). Female peer mentors early in college increase women's positive academic experiences and retention in engineering. Proceedings of the National Academy of Sciences, *114*(23), 5964–5969.

Duncombe, C., & Cassidy, M. (2016). Increasingly separate but unequal schools in U.S. and Virginia Schools. The Commonwealth Institute. 1–3.

Eaton, A. A., Saunders, J. F., Jacobson, R. K., & West, K. (2020). How gender and race stereotypes impact the advancement of scholars in STEM: Professors' biased evaluations of physics and biology post-doctoral candidates. *Sex Roles, 82*(3–4), 127–141.

Eccles, J. (2009). Who am I and what am I going to do with my life? Personal and collective identities as motivators of action. *Educational Psychologist, 44*(2), 78–89.

Eccles, J. S., Midgley, C., Wigfield, A., Buchanan, C. M., Reuman, D., Flanagan, C. et al. (1993). Development during adolescence: The impact of stage–environment fit on young adolescents' experiences in schools and in families. *American Psychologist, 48*, 90–101.

Erikson, E. H. (1968). Identity, youth, and crisis. New York: Norton.

Espinosa, L. (2011). Pipelines and pathways: Women of color in undergraduate STEM majors and the college experiences that contribute to persistence. *Harvard Educational Review, 81*(2), 209–241.

Estrada, M., Eppig, A., Flores, L., & Matsui, J. (2019). A longitudinal study of the biology scholars program: Maintaining student integration and intention to persist in science career pathways. *Understanding Interventions, 10* (1), 1–26.

Estrada, M., Hernandez, P. R., & Schultz, P. W. (2018). A longitudinal study of how quality mentorship and research experience integrate underrepresented minorities into STEM careers. *CBE – Life Sciences Education, 17* (1), ar9.

Estrada, M., Woodcock, A., Hernandez, P. R., & Schultz, P. W. (2011). Toward a model of social influence that explains minority student integration into the scientific community. *Journal of Educational Psychology, 103*(1), 206–222.

Farrell, L., & McHugh, L. (2017). Examining gender-STEM bias among STEM and non-STEM students using the Implicit Relational Assessment Procedure (IRAP). *Journal of Contextual Behavioral Science, 6*(1), 80–90.

Farrell, L., & McHugh, L. (2020). Exploring the relationship between implicit and explicit gender-STEM bias and behavior among STEM students using the Implicit Relational Assessment Procedure. *Journal of Contextual Behavioral Science, 15*, 142–152.

Fassinger, R. E., & Asay, P. A. (2006). Career counseling for women in science, technology, engineering, and mathematics (STEM) fields. *Handbook of Career Counseling for Women, 2*, 427–452.

Fayer, S., Lacey A., & Watson, A. (2017). *BLS spotlight on statistics: STEM occupations – past, present, and future*. Washington, DC: US Department of Labor, Bureau of Labor. www.bls.gov/spotlight/archive.htm

Fazio, R. H., & Zanna, M. P. (1981). Direct experience and attitude-behavior consistency. In L. Berkowitz, ed. *Advances in Experimental Social Psychology* (vol. 14, pp. 161–202). San Diego, CA: Academic Press.

Findley–Van Nostrand, D., & Pollenz, R. S. (2017). Evaluating psychosocial mechanisms underlying STEM persistence in undergraduates: Evidence of impact from a six-day pre–college engagement STEM academy program. *CBE – Life Sciences Education, 16*(2), ar36.

Finkel, L. (2017). Walking the path together from high school to STEM majors and careers: Utilizing community engagement and a focus on teaching to increase opportunities for URM students. *Journal of Science Education and Technology, 26*(1), 116–126.

Finn, J. D. (1989). Withdrawing from school. *Review of Educational Research, 59*(2), 117–142.

Fiske, S. T., & Taylor, S. E. (1991). *Social cognition*. New York: McGraw-Hill Book Company.

Foertsch, J., Alexander, B. B., & Penberthy, D. (2000). Summer research opportunity programs (SROPs) for minority undergraduates: A longitudinal study of program outcomes, 1986–1996. *Council of Undergraduate Research Quarterly, 20*(3), 114–119.

Foor, C. E., Walden, S. E., & Trytten, D. A. (2007). "I wish that I belonged more in this whole engineering group": Achieving individual diversity. *Journal of Engineering Education, 96*(2), 103–115.

Freeman, T. M., Anderman, L. H., & Jensen, J. M. (2007). Sense of belonging in college freshmen at the classroom and campus levels. *The Journal of Experimental Education, 75*(3), 203–220.

Fries-Britt, S. L., Younger, T. K., & Hall, W. D. (2010). Lessons from high-achieving students of color in physics. *New Directions for Institutional Research* (148), 75–83.

Gasiewski, J. A., Eagan, M. K., Garcia, G. A., Hurtado, S., & Chang, M. J. (2012). From gatekeeping to engagement: A multicontextual, mixed method study of student academic engagement in introductory STEM courses. *Research in Higher Education, 53*(2), 229–261.

Gates, A. (2019). The protégé effect in the retention of underrepresented minority undergraduate teaching assistants in geoscience: Preliminary indications from Newark, New Jersey. *Journal of Geoscience Education, 67*(4), 417–426.

Gates, A. E., & Kalczynski, M. J. (2016). The oil game: Generating enthusiasm for geosciences in urban youth in Newark, NJ. *Journal of Geoscience Education, 64*(1), 17–23.

Gati, I., & Asher, I. (2001). Prescreening, in-depth exploration, and choice: From decision theory to career counseling practice. *The Career Development Quarterly, 50*(2), 140–157.

Gawronski, B., & Payne, B. K. (Eds.). (2011). *Handbook of implicit social cognition: Measurement, theory, and applications.* New York: Guilford Press.

Gilmer, T. (2007). An understanding of the improved grades, retention and graduation rates of STEM majors at the Academic Investment in Math and Science (AIMS) Program of Bowling Green State University (BGSU). *Journal of STEM Education, 8* (1).

Graham, K. J., McIntee, E. J., Raigoza, A. F., Fazal, M. A., & Jakubowski, H. V. (2016). Activities in an S-STEM program to catalyze early entry into research. *Journal of Chemical Education, 94*(2), 177–182.

Graham, M. J., Frederick, J., Byars-Winston, A., Hunter, A. B., & Handelsman, J. (2013). Increasing persistence of college students in STEM. *Science, 341*(6153), 1455–1456.

Greenaway, K., Amiot, C. E., Louis, W. R., & Bentley, S. V. (2017). The role of psychological need satisfaction in promoting student identification. In K. I. Mavor, M. J. Platow, & B. Bizumic (Eds.), *Self and social identity in educational contexts* (pp. 176–192). Abingdon: Routledge/Taylor & Francis Group.

Greenwald, A. G., & Banaji, M. R. (1995). Implicit social cognition: Attitudes, self-esteem, and stereotypes. *Psychological Review, 102,* 4–27.

Griffith, A. L. (2010). Persistence of women and minorities in STEM field majors: Is it the school that matters? *Economics of Education Review, 29* (6), 911–922.

Grossman, J. M., & Porche, M. V. (2014). Perceived gender and racial/ethnic barriers to STEM success. *Urban Education, 49*(6), 698–727.

Haeger, H., & Fresquez, C. (2016). Mentoring for inclusion: The impact of mentoring on undergraduate researchers in the sciences. *CBE – Life Sciences Education, 15* (3), ar36.

Harmon-Jones, E., Harmon-Jones, C., & Price, T. F. (2013). What is approach motivation?. *Emotion Review, 5*(3), 291–295.

Hausmann, L. R., Schofield, J. W., & Woods, R. L. (2007). Sense of belonging as a predictor of intentions to persist among African American and White first-year college students. *Research in Higher Education, 48*(7), 803–839.

Hernandez, P. R., Schultz, P., Estrada, M., Woodcock, A., & Chance, R. C. (2013). Sustaining optimal motivation: A longitudinal analysis of interventions to broaden participation of underrepresented students in STEM. *Journal of Educational Psychology, 105*(1), 89.

Hernandez-Matias, L., Pérez-Donato, L., Román, P. L., Laureano-Torres, F., Calzada-Jorge, N., Mendoza, S., Washington, A. V., & Borrero, M. (2019). An exploratory study comparing students' science identity perceptions derived from a hands-on research and nonresearch-based summer learning experience. *Biochemistry and Molecular Biology Education, 48*, 134–142.

Herrera, F. A., Hurtado, S., Garcia, G. A., & Gasiewski, J. (2012). A model for redefining STEM identity for talented STEM graduate students. Paper Presented at the American Educational Research Association Annual Conference, Vancouver, BC.

Hidi, S., & Renninger, K. A. (2006). The four-phase model of interest development. *Educational Psychologist, 41*(2), 111–127.

Hogg, M. A., & Reid, S. A. (2006). Social identity, self-categorization, and the communication of group norms. *Communication Theory, 16*(1), 7–30.

Hulton, C. (2019). Using role models to increase diversity in STEM: The American workforce needs every capable STEM worker to keep America in a global leadership position. *Technology and Engineering Teacher, 79*(3), 16.

Hurtado, S., Cabrera, N. L., Lin, M. H., Arellano, L., & Espinosa, L. L. (2009). Diversifying science: Underrepresented student experiences in structured research programs. *Research in Higher Education, 50*(2), 189–214.

Hurtado, S., & Carter, D. F. (1997). Effects of college transition and perceptions of the campus racial climate on Latino college students' sense of belonging. *Sociology of Education, 70*, 324–345.

Hurtado, S., Carter, D. F., & Spuler, A. (1996). Latino student transition to college: Assessing difficulties and factors in successful college adjustment. *Research in Higher Education, 37*(2), 135–157.

Hurtado, S., Eagan, M. K., Tran, M. C., Newman, C. B., Chang, M. J., & Velasco, P. (2011). We do science here: Underrepresented students' interactions with faculty in different college contexts. *Journal of Social Issues, 67,* 553–579

Hurtado, S., Newman, C. B., Tran, M. C., & Chang, M. J. (2010). Improving the rate of success for underrepresented racial minorities in STEM fields: Insights from a national project. *New Directions for Institutional Research, 2010*(148), 5–15.

Inkelas, K. (2008). *National study of living-learning programs: 2007 report of findings.* College Park: University of Maryland.

Iyer, A., Jetten, J., Tsivrikos, D., Postmes, T., & Haslam, S. A. (2009). The more (and the more compatible) the merrier: Multiple group memberships and identity compatibility as predictors of adjustment after life transitions. *British Journal of Social Psychology, 48*(4), 707–733.

Jetten, J., Iyer, A., Tsivrikos, D., & Young, B. M. (2008). When is individual mobility costly? The role of economic and social identity factors. *European Journal of Social Psychology, 38*(5), 866–879.

Johnson, D. R. (2012). Campus racial climate perceptions and overall sense of belonging among racially diverse women in STEM majors. *Journal of College Student Development, 53*(2), 336–346.

Kamangar, F., Silver, G. B., Hohmann, C., Mehravaran, S., & Sheikhattari, P. (2019), Empowering Undergraduate Students to Lead Research: The ASCEND Program at Morgan State University. Broadening Participation in STEM (Diversity in Higher Education, Vol. 22), Emerald Publishing Limited, pp. 35–53.

Kaplan, A., & Flum, H. (2010). Achievement goal orientations and identity formation styles. *Educational Research Review, 5*(1), 50–67.

Kellow, J. T., & Jones, B. D. (2008). The effects of stereotypes on the achievement gap: Reexamining the academic performance of African American high school students. *Journal of Black Psychology, 34*(1), 94–120.

Kelman, H. C. (2006). Interests, relationships, identities: Three central issues for individuals and groups in negotiating their social environment. *Annual Review of Psychology, 57,* 1–26.

Kim, A. Y., Sinatra, G. M., & Seyranian, V. (2018). Developing a STEM identity among young women: A social identity perspective. *Review of Educational Research, 88*(4), 589–625.

Kram, K. E. (1985). *Mentoring at work: Developmental relationships in organizational life.* Glenview, IL: Scott Foresman.

Kuchynka, S., Findley-Van Nostrand, D., & Pollenz, R. S. (2019). Evaluating psychosocial mechanisms underlying STEM persistence in undergraduates: Scalability and longitudinal analysis of three cohorts from a six-day pre–college engagement STEM academy program. *CBE – Life Sciences Education, 18* (3), ar41.

Kuchynka, S., Reifsteck, T., Gates, A., & Rivera, L. M. (2020). Mechanisms the promote science identity among underrepresented minority students: A longitudinal investigation. Unpublished manuscript.

Kuchynka, S. L., Salomon, K., Bosson, J. K., El-Hout, M., Kiebel, E., Cooperman, C., & Toomey, R. (2018). Hostile and benevolent sexism and college women's STEM outcomes. *Psychology of Women Quarterly, 42*(1), 72–87.

Kunnen, E. S., Sappa, V., van Geert, P. L., & Bonica, L. (2008). The shapes of commitment development in emerging adulthood. *Journal of Adult Development, 15* (3–4), 113–131.

Labov, J. B. (2004). From the National Academies: The challenges and opportunities for improving undergraduate science education through introductory courses. *Cell Biology Education, 3*(4), 212–214.

Lacy, K. (2015). Race, privilege and the growing class divide. *Ethnic and Racial Studies, 38*(8), 1246–1249.

Lawner, E. K., Quinn, D. M., Camacho, G., Johnson, B. T., & Pan-Weisz, B. (2019). Ingroup role models and underrepresented students' performance and interest in STEM: A meta-analysis of lab and field studies. *Social Psychology of Education, 22*(5), 1169–1195.

Lee, O., & Buxton, C. A. (2010). *Diversity and equity in science education: Research, policy, and practice.* Multicultural Education Series. *Teachers College Press.*

Lee, O., & Luykx, A. (2006). *Science education and student diversity: Synthesis and research agenda.* Cambridge: Cambridge University Press.

Leach, C. W., Van Zomeren, M., Zebel, S., Vliek, M. L., Pennekamp, S. F., Doosje, B. Ouwerkerk, J., & Spears, R. (2008). Group-level self-definition and self-investment: A hierarchical (multicomponent) model of in-group identification. *Journal of Personality and Social Psychology, 95*(1), 144–165.

Lent, R. W., Brown, S. D., & Hackett, G. (1994). Toward a unifying social cognitive theory of career and academic interest, choice, and performance. *Journal of Vocational Behavior, 45*(1), 79–122.

Lent, R. W., Miller, M. J., Smith, P. E., Watford, B. A., Lim, R. H., & Hui, K. (2016). Social cognitive predictors of academic persistence and performance in engineering: Applicability across gender and race/ethnicity. *Journal of Vocational Behavior, 94*, 79–88.

Lewis, B. F. (2003). A critique of the literature on the underrepresentation of African Americans in science: Directions for future research. *Journal of Women and Minorities in Science and Engineering, 9*, 361–373.

Lisberg, A., & Woods, B. (2018). Mentorship, mindset and learning strategies: An integrative approach to increasing underrepresented minority student retention in a STEM undergraduate program. *Journal of STEM Education 19*(3), 14–20.

Liu, S. (2018). Entering the STEM pipeline: Exploring the impacts of a summer bridge program on students' readiness. *Journal of College Student Development, 59*(5), 635–640.

Luhtanen, R., & Crocker, J. (1992). A collective self-esteem scale: Self-evaluation of one's social identity. *Personality and Social Psychology Bulletin, 18*(3), 302–318.

Luyckx, K., Goossens, L., Soenens, B., & Beyers, W. (2006). Unpacking commitment and exploration: Preliminary validation of an integrative model of late adolescent identity formation. *Journal of Adolescence, 29*(3), 361–378.

Luyckx, K., Schwartz, S. J., Berzonsky, M. D., Soenens, B., Vansteenkiste, M., Smits, I., & Goossens, L. (2008). Capturing ruminative exploration: Extending the four-dimensional model of identity formation in late adolescence. *Journal of Research in Personality, 42*(1), 58–82.

Luyckx, K., Vansteenkiste, M., Goossens, L., & Duriez, B. (2009). Basic need satisfaction and identity formation: Bridging self-determination theory and process-oriented identity research. *Journal of Counseling Psychology, 56*(2), 276–288.

Mahoney, J. L., & Cairns, R. B. (1997). Do extracurricular activities protect against early school dropout?. *Developmental Psychology, 33*(2), 241–253.

Major, B., Spencer, S. J., Schmader, T., Wolfe, C., & Crocker, J. (1998). Coping with negative stereotypes about intellectual performance: The role of psychological disengagement. *Personality and Social Psychology Bulletin, 24*(1), 34–50.

Malik, J. A. N. (2014). STEM mentoring initiative moves forward. *Mrs Bulletin, 39*(8), 656–657. http://US2020.org.

Malone, K., & Barbino, G. (2009). Narrations of race in STEM research settings: Identity formation and its discontents. *Science Education, 93*(3), 485–510.

Maltese, A. V., & Tai, R. H. (2011). Pipeline persistence: Examining the association of educational experiences with earned degrees in STEM among US students. *Science Education, 95*(5), 877–907.

Mangu, D. M., Lee, A. R., Middleton, J. A., & Nelson, J. K. (2015, October). Motivational factors predicting STEM and engineering career intentions for high school students. IEEE Frontiers in Education Conference (FIE) (pp. 1–8).

Marcia, J. E. (1994). Ego identity and object relations. In J. M. Masling & R. F. Bornstein (Eds.), *Empirical perspectives on object relations theory* (pp. 59–103). Washington, DC: American Psychological Association.

Markus, H., & Nurius, P. (1986). Possible selves. *American Psychologist, 41*(9), 954–969.

Master, A., Cheryan, S., & Meltzoff, A. N. (2016). Computing whether she belongs: Stereotypes undermine girls' interest and sense of belonging in computer science. *Journal of Educational Psychology, 108*(3), 424.

Maton, K. I., Beason, T. S., Godsay, S., Sto. Domingo, M. R., Bailey, T. C., Sun, S., & Hrabowski, F. A. (2016). Outcomes and processes in the Meyerhoff scholars program: STEM PhD completion, sense of community, perceived program benefit, science identity, and research self-efficacy. *CBE –Life Sciences Education, 15* (3), ar48.

Maton, K. I., Hrabowski, F. A., & Ozdemir, M. (2007). Opening an African American STEM program to talented students of all races: Evaluation of the Meyerhoff Scholars Program, 1991–2005. In G. Orfield, P. Marin, S. M. Flores, & L. M. Garces (Eds.), *Charting the Future of College Affirmative Action: Legal Victories, Continuing Attacks, and New Research* (pp. 125–156). Los Angeles, CA: The Civil Rights Project, UCLA.

Maton, K. I., Pollard, S. A., McDougall Weise, T. V., & Hrabowski, F. A. (2012). Meyerhoff Scholars Program: A strengths-based, institution-wide approach to increasing diversity in science, technology, engineering, and mathematics. *Mount Sinai Journal of Medicine: A Journal of Translational and Personalized Medicine, 79*(5), 610–623.

Matsui, J., Liu, R., & Kane, C. M. (2003). Evaluating a science diversity program at UC Berkeley: More questions than answers. *Cell Biology Education, 2*(2), 117–121.

May, G. S., & Chubin, D. E. (2003). A retrospective on undergraduate engineering success for underrepresented minority students. *Journal of Engineering Education, 92*(1), 27–39.

McCarron, G. P., & Inkelas, K. K. (2006). The gap between educational aspirations and attainment for first-generation college students and the role of parental involvement. *Journal of College Student Development, 47*(5), 534–549.

McDonald, M. M., Zeigler-Hill, V., Vrabel, J. K., & Escobar, M. (2019). A single-item measure for assessing STEM identity. *Frontiers in Education, 4*, 78.

Meier, S. T., & Schmeck, R. R. (1985). The burned-out college student: A descriptive profile. *Journal of College Student Personnel, 26*, 63–69.

Mondisa, J. L., & McComb, S. A. (2015). Social community: A mechanism to explain the success of STEM minority mentoring programs. *Mentoring & Tutoring: Partnership in Learning, 23*(2), 149–163.

Morgenroth, T., Ryan, M. K., & Peters, K. (2015). The motivational theory of role modeling: How role models influence role aspirants' goals. *Review of General Psychology, 19*(4), 465–483.

National Academies of Sciences, Engineering, and Medicine (2007). *Rising above the gathering storm: Energizing and employing America for a brighter economic future.* Washington, DC: National Academies Press.
    (2019). *The Science of Effective Mentorship in STEM.* Washington, DC: The National Academies Press.

National Research Council. (2011).*Research training in the biomedical, behavioral, and clinical research sciences.* Washington, DC: National Academies Press.

National Science Board. (2015). *Revisiting the STEM workforce, A companion to science and engineering indicators 2014.* Arlington, VA: National Science Foundation.

National Science Foundation (2005). *Broadening participation through a comprehensive, integrated system.* Arlington, VA: National Science Foundation.
    (2019). *Women, minorities, and persons with disabilities in science and engineering: 2019.* National Center for Science and Engineering Statistics. Special Report NSF 19–304. Alexandria, VA: National Science Foundation.

Newell, D. C., Fletcher, S. L., & Anderson-Rowland, M. R. (2002). The women in applied science and engineering program: How diversified programming increases participation. American Society for Engineering Education Annual Conference, Montreal, Quebec, Canada, *7*, 1–9.

Oakes, J. (1990). Multiplying inequalities: The effects of race, social class, and tracking on opportunities to learn mathematics and science. Santa Monica, CA: The Rand Corporation (Report R-3928-NSF).

Olson, S., & Fagen, A. (2007). *Understanding interventions that encourage minorities to pursue research careers: Summary of a workshop.* Washington, DC: National Academies Press.

Ong, M. (2005). Body projects of young women of color in physics: Intersections of gender, race, and science. *Social Problems, 52*(4), 593–617.

Osborne, J. W., & Jones, B. D. (2011). Identification with academics and motivation to achieve in school: How the structure of the self influences academic outcomes. *Educational Psychology Review, 23*(1), 131–158.

Ostrove, J. M., & Long, S. M. (2007). Social class and belonging: Implications for college adjustment. *The Review of Higher Education, 30*(4), 363–389.

Pascarella, E. T., & Terenzini, P. T. (1983). Predicting voluntary freshman year persistence/withdrawal behavior in a residential university: A path analytic validation of Tinto's model. *Journal of Educational Psychology, 75*(2), 215–226.

Pender, M., Marcotte, D. E., Domingo, M. R. S., & Maton, K. I. (2010). The STEM pipeline: The role of summer research experience in minority students' Ph.D. aspirations. *Education Policy Analysis Archives*, *18*(30), 1–36.

Perez, T., Cromley, J. G., & Kaplan, A. (2014). The role of identity development, values, and costs in college STEM retention. *Journal of Educational Psychology*, *106*(1), 315–329.

Persaud, A., & Freeman, A. L. (2005). Creating a successful model for minority students' success in engineering: The PREF Summer Bridge Program. In 2005 Women in Engineering ProActive Network/National Association of Multicultural Engineering Program Advocates Joint Conference, held April 10–13, 2005, in Las Vegas, NV (pp. 1–7).

Pfund, C., Byars-Winston, A., Branchaw, J., Hurtado, S., & Eagan, K. (2016). Defining attributes and metrics of effective research mentoring relationships. *AIDS and Behavior*, *20*(2), 238–248.

Phinney, J. S., Torres Campos, C. M., Padilla Kallemeyn, D. M., & Kim, C. (2011). Processes and outcomes of a mentoring program for Latino college freshmen. *Journal of Social Issues*, *67*(3), 599–621.

Postmes, T., Baray, G., Haslam, S. A., Morton, T. A., & Swaab, R. I. (2006). The dynamics of personal and social identity formation. In T. Postmes & J. Jetten (Eds.), *Individuality and the group: Advances in social identity* (pp. 215–236). London: Sage Publications. https://doi.org/10.4135/9781446211946.n12

Pritchard, T. J., Perazzo, J. D., Holt, J. A., Fishback, B. P., McLaughlin, M., Bankston, K. D., & Glazer, G. (2016). Evaluation of a summer bridge: Critical component of the Leadership 2.0 Program. *Journal of Nursing Education*, *55*(4), 196–202.

Purdie-Vaughns, V., & Eibach, R. P. (2008). Intersectional invisibility: The distinctive advantages and disadvantages of multiple subordinate-group identities. *Sex Roles: A Journal of Research*, *59* (5–6), 377–391.

Quitadamo, I. J., Brahler, C. J., & Crouch, G. J. (2009). Peer-led team learning: A prospective method for increasing critical thinking in undergraduate science courses. *Science Educator*, *18*(1), 29–39.

Raelin, J. A., Bailey, M., Hamann, J., Pendleton, L., Reisberg, R., & Whitman, D. (2015). The role of work experience and self-efficacy in STEM student selection. *Journal of Excellence in College Teaching*, *26*(4), 29–50.

Ragins, B. R. (2012). Mentoring. In K. S. Cameron & G. M. Spreitzer (Eds.), *Oxford library of psychology. The Oxford handbook of positive organizational scholarship* (pp. 519–536). New York: Oxford University Press.

Ramsey, L. R., Betz, D. E., & Sekaquaptewa, D. (2013). The effects of an academic environment intervention on science identification among women in STEM. *Social Psychology of Education*, *16*(3), 377–397.

Rankin, S. R., & Reason, R. D. (2005). Differing perceptions: How students of color and white students perceive campus climate for underrepresented groups. *Journal of College Student Development, 46*(1), 43–61.

Reason, R. D. (2003). Student variables that predict retention: Recent research and new developments. *Naspa Journal, 40*(4), 172–191.

Rendón, L. I., Garcia, M., & Person, D. (2004). *Transforming the first year of college for students of color. The First-Year Experience Monograph Series No. 38.* National Resource Center for The First-Year Experience and Students in Transition. University of South Carolina, 1728 College Street, Columbia, SC 29208.

Renninger, K. A. (2009). Interest and identity development in instruction: An inductive model. *Educational Psychologist, 44*(2), 105–118.

Reyes, M. A., Anderson-Rowland, M. R., & McCartney, M. A. (1999, November). Student success: What factors influence persistence? *FIE '99 Frontiers in Education*, 29th Annual Frontiers in Education Conference. Designing the Future of Science and Engineering Education. Conference Proceedings (IEEE Cat. No. 99CH37011 (Vol. 1, pp. 11A5-21).

Richard, O. C. (2000). Racial diversity, business strategy, and firm performance: A resource-based view. *Academy of Management Journal, 43*(2), 164–177.

Robbins, S. B., Allen, J., Casillas, A., Peterson, C. H., & Le, H. (2006). Unraveling the differential effects of motivational and skills, social, and self-management measures from traditional predictors of college outcomes. *Journal of Educational Psychology, 98*(3), 598–616.

Rogers, W. D., & Ford, R. (1997). Factors that affect student attitude toward biology. *Bioscene, 23*(2), 3–5.

Rosenthal, L., London, B., Levy, S. R., & Lobel, M. (2011). The roles of perceived identity compatibility and social support for women in a single-sex STEM program at a co-educational university. *Sex Roles, 65* (9–10), 725–736.

Schwab, K., & Sala-i-Martín, X. (2012). *The Global Competitiveness Report 2012–2013 of the World Economic Forum (full data edition)*. Geneva: World Economic Forum.

Schwartz, S. J. (2001). The evolution of Eriksonian and neo-Eriksonian identity theory and research: A review and integration. *Identity: An International Journal of Theory and Research, 1*, 7–58.

Schweiger, D. M., & Denisi, A. S. (1991). Communication with employees following a merger: A longitudinal field experiment. *Academy of Management Journal, 34*(1), 110–135.

Seymour, E., & Hewitt, N. M. (1997). *Talking about leaving: Why undergraduates leave the sciences*. Boulder, CO: Westview.

Shaw, E. J., & Barbuti, S. (2010). Patterns of persistence in intended college major with a focus on STEM majors. *NACADA Journal, 30*(2), 19–34.

Slovacek, S. P., Whittinghill, J. C., Tucker, S., Rath, K. A., Peterfreund, A. R., Kuehn, G. D., & Reinke, Y. G. (2011). Minority students severely underrepresented in science, technology, engineering, and math. *Journal of STEM Education: Innovations and Research, 12* (1).

Soldner, M., Rowan-Kenyon, H., Inkelas, K. K., Garvey, J., & Robbins, C. (2012). Supporting students' intentions to persist in STEM disciplines: The role of living-learning programs among other social-cognitive factors. *The Journal of Higher Education, 83*(3), 311–336.

Spencer, S. J., Logel, C., & Davies, P. G. (2016). Stereotype threat. *Annual Review of Psychology, 67*, 415–437.

Swim, J. K., Hyers, L. L., Cohen, L. L., Fitzgerald, D. C., & Bylsma, W. H. (2003). African American college students' experiences with everyday racism: Characteristics of and responses to these incidents. *Journal of Black Psychology, 29*(1), 38–67.

Starr, C. R. (2018). "I'm not a science nerd!" STEM stereotypes, identity, and motivation among undergraduate women. *Psychology of Women Quarterly, 42*(4), 489–503.

Steele, C. M. (1997). A threat in the air: How stereotypes shape intellectual identity and performance. *American Psychologist, 52*(6), 613–629.

Stephen, J., Fraser, E., & Marcia, J. E. (1992). Moratorium-achievement (Mama) cycles in lifespan identity development: Value orientations and reasoning system correlates. *Journal of Adolescence, 15*(3), 283–300.

Stout, J. G., Dasgupta, N., Hunsinger, M., & McManus, M. A. (2011). STEMing the tide: Using ingroup experts to inoculate women's self-concept in science, technology, engineering, and mathematics (STEM). *Journal of Personality and Social Psychology, 100*(2), 255–270.

Strayhorn, T. L. (2011). Bridging the pipeline: Increasing underrepresented students' preparation for college through a summer bridge program. *American Behavioral Scientist, 55*(2), 142–159.

(2015). Reframing academic advising for student success: From advisor to cultural navigator. *The Journal of the National Academic Advising Association, 35*(1), 56–63.

(2018). *College students' sense of belonging: A key to educational success for all students*. Routledge.

Swann, W. B., & Bosson, J. K. (2010). Self and identity. In S. T. Fiske, D. T. Gilbert, & G. Lindzey (Eds.), *Handbook of social psychology* (5th ed., pp. 589–628). New York, NY: McGraw-Hill.

Syed, M., Azmitia, M., & Cooper, C. R. (2011). Identity and academic success among underrepresented ethnic minorities: An interdisciplinary review and integration. *Journal of Social Issues, 67*(3), 442–468.

Tai, R. H., Liu, C. Q., Maltese, A. V., & Fan, X. (2006). Planning early for careers in science. Science, 312, 1143–1144.

Tajfel, H. (1978). The achievement of intergroup differentiation. In H. Tajfel (Ed.), *Differentiation between social categories: Studies in social psychology* (pp. 77–98). London: Academic Press.

(1981). *Human groups and social categories: Studies in social psychology.* Cambridge: Cambridge University Press.

(1982). Social psychology of intergroup relations. *Annual Review of Psychology, 33*(1), 1–39.

Tajfel, H., & Turner, J. C. (1979). An Integrative theory of intergroup conflict. In W. G. Austin & S. Worchel (Eds.), *The social psychology of inter-group relations* (pp. 33–47). Monterey, CA: Brooks/Cole.

(1986). The social identity theory of intergroup behaviour. In S. Worchel, & W. G. Austin (Eds.), *Psychology of intergroup relations* (pp. 7–24). Chicago: Nelson-Hall.

Tenenbaum, H., Crosby, F. J., & Gliner, M. D. (2001). Mentoring relationships in graduate school. *Journal of Vocational Behavior, 59*(3), 326–341.

Tenenbaum, L. S., Anderson, M. K., Jett, M., & Yourick, D. L. (2014). An innovative near-peer mentoring model for undergraduate and secondary students: STEM focus. *Innovative Higher Education, 39*(5), 375–385.

Tinto, V. (1975). Dropout from higher education: A theoretical synthesis of recent re- search. *Review of Educational Research, 45,* 89–125.

(1987). *Leaving college: Rethinking the causes and cures of student attrition.* Chicago: University of Chicago Press.

(1988). Stages of student departure: Reflections on the longitudinal character of student leaving. *Journal of Higher Education, 59,* 438–455.

Tenenbaum, H., Crosby, F. J., & Gliner, M. D. (2001). Mentoring relationships in graduate school. *Journal of Vocational Behavior* 59 (3), 326–341.

Tomasko, D. L., Ridgway, J. S., Waller, R. J., & Olesik, S. V. (2016). Association of summer bridge program outcomes with STEM retention of targeted demographic groups. *Journal of College Science Teaching, 45*(4), 90–99.

Toven-Lindsey, B., Levis-Fitzgerald, M., Barber, P. H., & Hasson, T. (2015). Increasing persistence in undergraduate science majors: A model for institutional support of underrepresented students. *CBE – Life Science Education, 14* (2), ar12.

Trujillo, G., Aguinaldo, P. G., Anderson, C., Bustamante, J., Gelsinger, D. R., Pastor, M. J. Wright. J., Márquez-Magaña. L., & Riggs, B. (2015). Near-peer

STEM mentoring offers unexpected benefits for mentors from traditionally underrepresented backgrounds. *Perspectives on Undergraduate Research and Mentoring: PURM, 4*(1).

Turner, J. C., Hogg, M. A., Oakes, P. J., Reicher, S. D., & Wetherell, M. S. (1987). *Rediscovering the social group: A self-categorization theory.* Oxford: Basil Blackwell.

Turner, J. C., Oakes, P. J., Haslam, S. A., & McGarty, C. (1994). Self and collective: Cognition and social context. *Personality and Social Psychology Bulletin, 20*(5), 454–463.

Turner, J. C., & Reynolds, K. J. (2011). Self-categorization theory. *Handbook of Theories in Social Psychology, 2*(1), 399–417.

Turner, J. C., Reynolds, K. J., Haslam, S. A., & Veenstra, K. E. (2006). Reconceptualizing personality: Producing individuality by defining the personal self. In T. Postmes & J. Jetten (Eds.), *Individuality and the group: Advances in social identity* (pp. 11–36). London: Sage.

Tyson, W., Lee, R., Borman, K. M., & Hanson, M. A. (2007). Science, technology, engineering, and mathematics (STEM) pathways: High school science and math coursework and postsecondary degree attainment. *Journal of Education for Students Placed at Risk, 12*(3), 243–270.

Valsiner, J. (1992). Interest: A metatheoretical perspective. In K.A. Renninger, S. Hidi, & A. Krapp (Eds.), *The role of interest in learning and development* (pp. 27–41). Hillsdale, NJ: Erlbaum.

Van Leuvan, P. (2004). Young women's science/mathematics career goals from seventh grade to high school graduation. *The Journal of Educational Research, 97*(5), 248–268.

Villarejo, M., Barlow, A. E., Kogan, D., Veazey, B. D., & Sweeney, J. K. (2008). Encouraging minority undergraduates to choose science careers: Career paths survey results. *CBE – Life Sciences Education, 7*(4), 394–409.

Walton, G. M., & Cohen, G. L. (2007). A question of belonging: Race, social fit, and achievement. *Journal of Personality and Social Psychology, 92*(1), 82–96.

(2011). A brief social-belonging intervention improves academic and health outcomes of minority students. *Science, 331*(6023), 1447–1451.

Wang, X. (2013). Why students choose STEM majors: Motivation, high school learning, and postsecondary context of support. *American Educational Research Journal, 50*(5), 1081–1121.

Watkins, J., & Mazur, E. (2013). Retaining students in science, technology, engineering, and mathematics (STEM) majors. *Journal of College Science Teaching, 42*(5), 36–41.

Wells, B., Sanchez, A., & Attridge, J. (2007). Modeling student interest in science, technology, engineering and mathematics. IEEE Summit. "Meeting the growing demand for engineers and their educators," Munich, Germany.

Wilson, A. R., & Leaper, C. (2016). Bridging multidimensional models of ethnic–racial and gender identity among ethnically diverse emerging adults. *Journal of Youth and Adolescence, 45*(8), 1614–1637.

Wilson, A. T., & Grigorian, S. (2019). The near-peer mathematical mentoring cycle: Studying the impact of outreach on high school students' attitudes toward mathematics. *International Journal of Mathematical Education in Science and Technology, 50*(1), 46–64.

Witkow, M. R., & Fuligni, A. J. (2011). Ethnic and generational differences in the relations between social support and academic achievement across the high school years. *Journal of Social Issues, 67*(3), 531–552.

Woodcock, A., Hernandez, P. R., Estrada, M., & Schultz, P. (2012). The consequences of chronic stereotype threat: Domain disidentification and abandonment. *Journal of Personality and Social Psychology, 103*(4), 635–646.

Yang, H. J. (2004). Factors affecting student burnout and academic achievement in multiple enrollment programs in Taiwan's technical-vocational colleges. *International Journal of Educational Development, 24*, 283–301.

Young, J., Ortiz, N., & Young, J. (2017). STEMulating interest: A meta-analysis of the effects of out-of-school time on student STEM interest. *International Journal of Education in Mathematics, Science and Technology, 5*(1), 62–74.

Cambridge Elements ≡

Applied Social Psychology

Susan Clayton
College of Wooster, Ohio
Susan Clayton is a social psychologist at the College of Wooster in Wooster, Ohio. Her research focuses on the human relationship with nature, how it is socially constructed, and how it can be utilized to promote environmental concern.

Editorial Board

About the Series
Many social psychologists have used their research to understand and address pressing social issues, from poverty and prejudice to work and health. Each Element in this series reviews a particular area of applied social psychology. Elements will also discuss applications of the research findings and describe directions for future study.

Cambridge Elements ≡

Applied Social Psychology

Elements in the Series

A full series listing is available at: www.cambridge.org/EASP

Printed in the United States
By Bookmasters